INDIAN LIFE
OF LONG AGO IN THE
CITY OF NEW YORK

MODEL OF INDIAN LIFE AT INWOOD, MANHATTAN

By Ned C. Burns

EXHIBITED AT THE MUSEUM OF THE CITY OF NEW YORK AND REPRODUCED THROUGH THEIR COURTESY

INDIAN LIFE OF LONG AGO IN THE CITY OF NEW YORK

BY
REGINALD PELHAM BOLTON

HONORARY MEMBER

NEW YORK HISTORICAL SOCIETY

MUSEUM OF THE AMERICAN INDIAN, HEYE FOUNDATION

MUSEUM OF THE CITY OF NEW YORK

AUTHOR OF

INDIAN PATHS IN THE GREAT METROPOLIS

NEW YORK CITY IN INDIAN POSSESSION

RELICS OF THE REVOLUTION

WITH ILLUSTRATIONS BY THE AUTHOR
AND PHOTOGRAPHS FROM THE ARCHIVES OF
THE MUSEUM OF THE AMERICAN INDIAN, HEYE FOUNDATION

THE MUSEUM OF THE CITY OF NEW YORK

Harmony books

DEDICATED TO
THE MEMORY
OF
ALANSON B. SKINNER

Enlarged Edition © 1972 by Crown Publishers, Inc.
© 1934 by Reginald Pelham Bolton
Library of Congress Card Catalog Number: 72-89363
ISBN: 0-517-501562
517-501562
Printed in the United States of America.
Published simultaneously in Canada by
General Publishing Company Limited.

PREFACE TO
THE SECOND EDITION

Some thirty-five years ago Reginald P. Bolton wrote *Indian Life of Long Ago in the City of New York* in an effort to bring together what was then understood about the subject at the time. Mr. Bolton had been active in educational and museum affairs, and knew the frequency with which questions about aboriginal life in this area came up in class and museum situations, and felt that a one-volume general survey would be useful. The book was an immediate success and, shortly after its appearance, it was out of print. As a consequence it is impossible to find copies of the book in used-book shops.

Since that date, very few books have appeared on the subject of early Indian inhabitants of New York City. There have been some excellent individual studies related to New York State prehistory, in which the matter of New York City settlements have been considered, but these have been more concerned with specific archeological sites than the generalized pattern of land use within the five boroughs. It is indeed surprising that so little concern has been expressed in this particular matter of the pre-European settlement of one of the major urban areas of the United States.

Even more curious is the absence of a sustained interest about the Indians of New York City, in spite of the existence of a large population of citizens of native ancestry in the five boroughs. Indeed, a favorite query has long been "Where was the largest Indian village in the United States?" simply to make the point that Brooklyn enjoyed that distinction for well over a generation; the number of Mohawk and other Indian peoples who settled around the Gowanus district established a primacy that has only recently been over-shadowed by Los Angeles, California.

Although we know a great deal more today about certain aspects of New York City in aboriginal times, the present work remains a remarkably useful compilation for general purposes. The author was himself a surprising person. Born in England in 1856, Bolton came to the United States and built a reputation as a construction engineer and buildings designer. For a hobby, he undertook the study of early New York history, and as one of the genre of gentlemen historians so familiar at the turn of the century, settled back to write up the history of the city. At the time of his death in 1942, he had the distinction of having a building in lower Manhattan named after him, and was the author of some fourteen books dealing with engineering matters and Indian history.

Although Bolton did considerable fieldwork in and around Manhattan, he was not a trained archeologist, and much of the results of his efforts have never been adequately studied or published. He was associated with the American Museum of Natural History, and the Museum of the American Indian, and his archeological collections are housed in those two institutions.

The present work is not without fault; many of the sources on which he had to depend have since been refined and honed by more extensive study, most particularly concerning our knowledge of early man in New York. Yet the general conclusions of his research hold up remarkably well today.

While there is certainly room for other works on the Indian, until such books appear, *Indian Life of Long Ago in the City of New York* will remain a serviceable and comprehensive survey of the early aboriginal period in New York, and the present reprint is a welcome addition to the small library on the subject.

Frederick J. Dockstader

Director

Museum of the American Indian

June 15, 1972   Heye Foundation

"THUS WAS MANHATTAN ISLAND AGAIN LEFT IN PRIMEVAL SOLITUDE, WAITING TILL COMMERCE SHOULD COME AND CLAIM ITS OWN." *PHOTOGRAPH COURTESY OF THE MUSEUM OF THE CITY OF NEW YORK*

INTRODUCTION

During the past decade this writer has received many inquiries for information regarding the prehistoric and early historic life of the Indians located in what is now the Greater City of New York. Although we have various accounts of these aboriginal inhabitants which were written by early historians, it has required deep research to find many of these references, and even when found, the fact that they have not been correlated has made their use most unsatisfactory.

Mr. Reginald Pelham Bolton, the author of the present volume, has devoted over thirty years of study to the question of the aboriginal inhabitants of the present City of New York, and it may be stated without question that there is no other individual who knows as much of the history and also of the artifacts of the former Indian residents of this city as does Mr. Bolton, he having excavated numerous prehistoric sites within the present city limits.

Fortunately Mr. Bolton has been prevailed upon by some of his friends to put these facts on paper, and the result is this work, which I feel confident will be welcomed not alone by adult students of the early history of New York City, but also by the younger enthusiasts of coming generations, as represented in such organizations as the Boy Scouts and the Camp Fire Girls, as well as pupils of schools in general.

Director,
Museum of the American Indian,
Heye Foundation.

PROLOGUE

Some time ago, a distinguished French authoress came to New York from Paris to see something of America. I had the pleasure of acting as her guide to Poe's little cottage at Fordham, and I inquired of her what other feature of American life was of particular interest to her. Her reply was, "Indians," and to see some of those original owners of the continent, it was her purpose to travel to the west.

It caused her some surprise when I stated that there were many American Indians in the City of New York, earning a living by quiet industry, and some of them taking part in the education of our children in the public schools.

I introduced the lady to an Indian woman, and to my surprise I soon heard them conversing in excellent French. My Indian friend had received her education in an Ursuline Convent of French-speaking Sisters, in the homelands of her tribe, the Cherokee.

That incident may indicate the fact which the story of Indian life in New York will illustrate,... that our native Americans, given the opportunities and facilities which have been enjoyed by the white or European settlers on this continent, would have absorbed this civilization, and would have made use of their increased knowledge, as well and perhaps better than those who came to their country armed with superior information, weapons, and methods of existence, by means of which the white man displaced the natives, nor did he disdain in so doing, treachery, ill-use, and force.

One of the least prejudiced accounts of native life in New York in early days was written by the Reverend Charles Wooley, a young priest of the Anglican Church, who spent two years in New York in 1678-90, and who, on his return to England wrote his reminiscences while still fresh in his memory. He was not hostile to the natives, as were Jonas Michaelius and other clerical observers, and he gained much of his information at first hand from a native named "Long Claus," an interpreter whose name appears as witness to deeds of sale of lands in the area of the present City, who was probably well-informed. Wolley criticized those "highflown Religionists who stile the Indians Populus Terrae and look upon them as a reprobate despicable sort of creature," and he found something to admire in their ways and doings, and much of interest in their accomplishments, as those who know the circumstances of their existence have also found.

I am hopeful that this assemblage of facts will enable the reader to regard the natives of New York in the same receptive manner, and to visualize them as they lived their lives before the white settlers brought those European methods and materials by means of which they became debauched and discredited.

Of the American Indians of the region in which this Great Metropolis, of varied nationalities, is now situated, we shall proceed to piece together the fragmentary facts recorded in history, and the story told by the relics of their life, left by them upon the sites of their old-time homes.

I desire to acknowledge the assistance which I have received in the preparation of this work from my kind and well-informed friends of the Museum of the American Indian, Heye Foundation—

Mr. George G. Heye, Director, for his reading of M. S., for many helpful suggestions thereon, and for his commendatory introduction.

Mr. William C. Orchard, for his expert advice and guidance on my drawings and illustrations.

Miss Ruth Gaines, Librarian of the Huntington Free Library, for her skilful reading and helpful criticism of the manuscript.

Reginald Pelham Bolton

CONTENTS

xvi

ILLUSTRATIONS

xviii

INDIAN LIFE
OF LONG AGO IN THE
CITY OF NEW YORK

"OUR INDIAN ALLIES—SIOUX WARRIORS MAKING PURCHASES ON BROADWAY FOR
THEMSELVES AND SQUAWS, OCTOBER 5TH, 1877." FROM FRANK LESLIE'S ILLUSTRATED
NEWSPAPER, OCTOBER 20, 1877. *PHOTOGRAPH COURTESY OF THE MUSEUM OF THE
CITY OF NEW YORK*

xx

I
THE BEGINNING OF THE LENAPE

THE natives of the American continent were named, by ignorant European visitors, "Indians," because the ship-masters and crews of their vessels supposed that the Atlantic coast was the shoreline of Asia, and that they were meeting, in the brown-skinned people of the new-found lands, the Hindus of Hindustan. If they had known anything of the languages of the two peoples, such a misunderstanding would not have been made. The name has clung to them ever since, though we have added by way of explanation, the European name of their country, and now describe the race as "American-Indian," a compound which has sometimes been wrought into a single word, "Amerind."

It is by their language that we are able to identify the nationality of those pre-historic people who in days preceding the advent of the European, occupied the area on which is now situated the vast metropolis.

As of old, when the apostle was called to account, we may say of the Lenape

"Thy speech betrayeth thee!"

or as the Herald cried at Dura

"O people—nations and languages."

1

The language, of which a number of words were recorded in written form by the law-scribes of the Dutch, was that which was used by the great tribe of the Lenape,* sometimes called the "Delaware" Nation.

Some of the Indian tribes of the eastern part of the United States had a tradition to the effect that their ancestors had migrated from another region. There is some confirmation of that tradition in the fact that the Unami Lenape of this region seem to have been preceded by a race of whose existence in several places, evidence has been found. These primeval people seem to have been unacquainted with the Lenape methods of shaping stones into smooth tools, finished weapons, and carefully prepared missiles, and their implements seem to have been pieces of bone and their weapons formed of the points of the antlers of deer. Their homes have been explored at several places within the area of the City, and indications of their existence have been found:

At Weir Creek, on Throg's Neck, in the Borough of the Bronx.

At Jamaica, on Long Island, in the Borough of Queens.

At the foot of Dyckman Street, in the Borough of Manhattan.

At Burial Ridge, Ward's Point, in the Borough of Richmond.

The first-named settlement was extensive and is important in affording evidence of the existence of these prehistoric natives.

The tribe of Lenape included chieftaincies on both sides of the Hudson, and around the waters of the harbor of New York.

The Hackinsack had their headquarters at Gamoenapa, our present Communipaw, and the territory they occupied included part of Staten Island. Their people were settled on land now occupied by Jersey City, Hoboken, Weehawken, Newark and Passaic.

They were related to the Tappan, whose lands extended from Hackensack River along the west side of the Hudson toward the Highland mountains, as far as Nayack, our present Nyack.

Part of the Tappan, or their relatives, the Aquacanonck, were

---

* Pronounced "Laynarpy."

2

settled at Paterson, and their settlements extended into the interior of northern New Jersey. North of Nayack we find the Rumackenanck or Haverstroo chieftaincy, probably a clan of the Minsi branch of the Lenape nation.

The southern part of Staten Island was occupied by the Sanhikan or Raritan chieftaincy. Their people were settled along the Raritan River far into the interior of New Jersey, and a branch of the Unami Lenape known as the Navasink, occupied the territory south of the Bay and also part of the nearby New Jersey shore.

From territory near Navasink river an important pathway led, which was known as "The Minisink Path." It extended westward to a crossing of the Raritan river near Perth Amboy, thence proceeding through the Short Hills towards the territory on which the Minisink or Minsi branch of the Lenape was settled.

The name "Lenape" thus inseparably connected with the earliest beginnings of human occupation of the area of the City of New York is derived from a combination of two words: the first being the word "eren", indicating *real, true* or *genuine,* the "R" having been gradually disused and "L" taking its place. The second syllable is "apeu" or "napeu", meaning a man, a male or by inference a human being.

The tribal title of "Lenape" thus indicated an original race of human beings, as distinguished perhaps from other offshoots of tribal form, not regarded as thoroughbreds.

There have been some interesting and divergent conjectures regarding the origin of the entire native race in the Americas. One of these surmises was to the effect that the race may have originated in certain navigators from China who are thought to have found their way across the Pacific Ocean to the continent of America some centuries before the beginning of the Christian era. Such a suggestion, however, presupposes that those indefinite navigators were settlers, and were accompanied by females, which does not appear to be probable. We may, however, leave the question of the

3

origin of the race in the Americas as one too remote for connection with the story of the natives inhabiting the area of the City of New York, and commence our record with the traditions of the Lenape as to their arrival in this region.

The tradition of that tribe was to the effect that the Lenape at one time resided in a region on the west or northwest of this continent, where great ice-covered waters were existent. This would indicate that their early home may have been in the region of the Great Lakes.

The "Walum Olum" or Painted Score, is a written interpretation of a pictograph or drawing which is said to have recorded the facts of a treasured legend or tradition of the Lenape nation.

A screed, recording the features of the picture, was obtained in 1820 from some member of the tribe, by a doctor of the name of Ward. The tribe at that time had removed west of New York and was then settled in Indiana. There is no doubt that each tribe had such traditions, but as they had no written form of language, the record of the meaning of this picture must have been made by some person acquainted with written characters, for the story derived from the Walum Olum was written down in Indian words.

The meaning as it reaches us would therefore appear to have been that of a record by a European from an interpretation by some native of the pictograph.

The pictorial tradition, inscribed and transcribed, was then translated by another writer,* by which means we reach the substance of the story, in the following form:

THE WALUM OLUM

After the rushing waters
The Lenape of the Turtle were close together in hollow homes.
It freezes where they abode
It snows, it storms, it is cold where they abode.

_____
* The Lenape and their Legends, D. G. Brinton, Philadelphia, 1885.

4

All the cabin fires of that land were disquieted
And all said to their priest
LET US GO.
On the wonderful slippery water
On the stone hard water
All went.
On the great Tidal Sea
The mussel-bearing Sea
They all come.
They tarry at the land of the Spruce Pines.
Those from the West
Come with hesitation
Esteeming highly their old home
At the Turtle Land."

If this story has come to us undistorted by its explanation and its translation, we have a picture of a hardy race living in a region of frost and snow, becoming discontented with the privations and hardships of their existence, and unanimously deciding upon an emigration to a more hospitable region, where food could more easily be obtained.

On their slow progress towards the coast they reach a land of forest, and linger there an indefinite period, during which another migration meets and joins with them, coming from the West and retaining a remembrance of their homeland in which the Turtle was their emblem or totem.

As to time or period of that migration and meeting, we know nothing, but the slow processes of development by a simple and uneducated race, into the methods of livelihood and into the system of society to which they had attained at the beginning of the seventeenth century, indicate the passage of a long period of time, probably more than hundreds, perhaps thousands of years, during which a prehistoric population which had before their arrival occupied the site of the future metropolis, was eking out a rude existence, and had by slow stages reached a certain stage of progress, when the Lenape immigration overwhelmed and probably absorbed

5

them. The cause of the widespread migration described in the legend may have been the dire lack of fuel supply, or it may have been the exhaustion of meat food in the country of their origin. Its direction towards New York was certainly due to information as to the abundance of sea food, and the ease of living conditions, in that locality.

In much the same manner the invasion of Palestine was conceived, and the fate of its unfortunate inhabitants may have been paralleled in the destruction of the prehistoric occupants of the City of New York.

The region in which they lived, which has now become the area of the greater City, was a paradise of nature, teeming with its products, and rich in natural beauty of woods and waters.

Its varied climate, as one old-time writer described it, was "of a Sweet and Wholesome Breath," its "uplands covered with berries, roots, chestnuts and walnuts, beach and oak masts." In the forest grew great oaks, "cedars, pines and firres." Birds sang in the branches, the deer and elk roamed the grassy meadows, the waters swarmed with fish, and the woods were redolent with the scent of the wild grape and of many flowers. Oak trees grew seventy feet high.

It is possible that, following Indian customs, the conquering race of the Lenape absorbed these prehistoric people by adopting them as members of their families. At the Weir Creek station we found in the lower layers of village rubbish, horn and bone tools and in the upper layers implements of stone. This circumstance confirms the idea that the same place was first used by unknown or prehistoric residents, and was at some time thereafter continued as a village after the Lenape had arrived.

On a site which was explored by Alanson Skinner, situated at the foot of Dyckman Street, by the Hudson River, he found in the lowest layers, crude implements of stone, lacking polish or smoothing, mingled with bones of the bear and of the elk, affording indications of the existence of ancient man on Manhattan Island among the wild creatures of primeval times.

The story of Indian origin and migration, told by the "Walum Olum," was to some extent confirmed by a relation to Alanson Skinner, of the same subject.

It formed part of a manuscript, the substance of which was described to him by a missionary. The story was written by a "Captain" Hendrick and appears to have been composed by that chieftain of the Mahican tribe about 1822. The M.S. was lost, but the substance of its story, as recalled by the missionary, was as follows:*

"The ancestors of the Mahicans, long ago, emigrated far from the west, where the waters ebb and flow. For some cause unknown, they migrated to the East, as far as the great western river." . . .

"While they lived on the Western River, an extraordinary famine happened, which obliged them to separate, and spread themselves in the wilderness of the East, for sustenance." . . .

"Advancing to the East they found many great waters, but none of them ebbed and flowed . . . until they came to the great river, now called the Hudson. When they saw this river they said one to another, 'this is like Muhheakunnuk, the place of our ancestors.' Finding that game was plenty, they concluded here to kindle a fire and hang a kettle, from which they and their children after them might dip out their daily refreshment."

This tradition, while it confirms the main feature of the migration of the Lenape race from the West, suffers from some distortion, because there is no river in the West which has any tide, and it would be necessary to assume, if the story were entirely reliable, that the migration crossed the entire continent from the tidal waters of the Pacific. That may, however, represent part of an older tradition, confirmatory of an original migration of the Indian race from Asia.

That the human race had occupied this continent and had found a livelihood, and had developed the use of fire, at a remote period

---

* Skinner, Mahikan Ethnology, 1925.

7

of perhaps fifteen thousand years ago, has been indicated by the discovery in the Middle West, of objects of human manipulation, and of the ashes of their fires, in association with the bones of the musk ox and other extinct creatures. We may reasonably assume therefore that the story told by the Painted Score of the origin of the Lenape in a western region, harks back to a remote date, and that their occupancy of the area of the Greater City covered a long period of time.

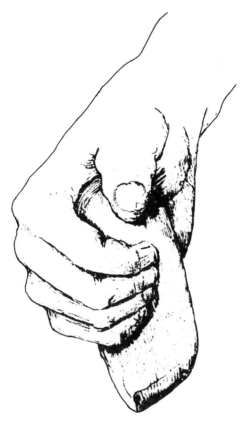

THE CELT

THE TOOL OF PRIMITIVE MAN

THE "CELT" IS A NAME APPLIED TO THE PRIMITIVE FORM OF CUTTING IMPLEMENT WHICH IS SUPPOSED TO HAVE BEEN THE EARLIEST TOOL USED BY MANKIND. IT WAS A NAME DERIVED FROM THE WELSH WORD "CELT" WHICH MEANS A FLINTY STONE, THOUGH SOME ATTRIBUTE IT TO THE LATIN WORD CELTIS, WHICH MEANS A CHISEL.

THE STONE, ROUGHLY BLOCKED INTO SHAPE, AND CHIPPED TO A CUTTING EDGE, WAS HELD IN THE HAND AS SHOWN, AND MUST HAVE BEEN WRAPPED IN SKIN, FOR OTHERWISE NO HAND, HOWEVER HORNY, COULD LONG WITHSTAND THE ABRASIVE EFFECT OF THE ROUGH SURFACE. THIS MAY HAVE BEEN THE INCENTIVE WHICH LED THE SUCCESSORS OF PALAEO-LITHIC MAN TO GRIND THE SURFACE OF THEIR TOOLS. CELTS OF MORE RECENT DATE ARE SOMETIMES HIGHLY POLISHED, AND SOME WERE PROBABLY FASTENED WITH RESIN IN WOODEN HANDLES.

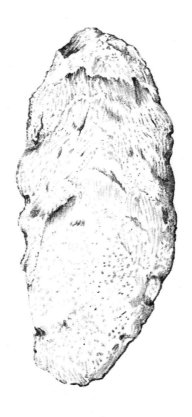

A PALAEOLITHIC CELT

THIS IS THE EARLIEST AND CRUDEST FORM OF CUTTING TOOL DEVISED BY MAN, AND IN THIS ROUGH AND UNPOLISHED CONDITION IT INDICATES A VERY EARLY ORIGIN, PROBABLY BEFORE THE NATIVES OF THE METRO-POLITAN REGION HAD LEARNED TO POLISH THEIR IMPLEMENTS, AND TO DEVISE SUCH AS COULD BE ATTACHED TO A HANDLE.

THAT PERIOD IN MAN'S EXISTENCE IS DESCRIBED AS THE NEOLITHIC AGE.

THIS CELT WAS FOUND BY WILLIAM L. CALVER IN A GRAVEL PIT, SITUATED SEVERAL FEET BELOW THE PRESENT SURFACE OF THE GROUND. THE LOCATION WAS ON HUNT'S POINT, IN THE BOROUGH OF THE BRONX.

8b

II
DIVISIONS AND TERRITORIES

THE natives occupying the site of the City of New York were divided into a number of chieftaincies. Their people settled in a certain locality, naturally selected their own leader, who became the Sachem or Chief of that locality. While, therefore, they continued to belong to the Lenape tribe, they came in time to be known by local or territorial names, and sometimes by the name of their Sachem.

These divisions are in some cases a matter of historical records, because in their transfers of land to white colonists, some of these clans or chieftaincies named the tract of land of which they were the occupants, or of which they considered themselves the proprietors. The outlines of these tracts were defined in writing in the legal conveyance which was prepared by the European purchasers, and in these records we get a picture of the boundaries of the several chieftaincies which occupied the site of the Greater City and of its surrounding territory. It was by the purchase of these tracts of land that many of our present townships came to be defined, and today we shall find the same or very similar tracts forming the counties, townships and boroughs of the modern city.

Thus within the City we find that Kings County, which is now the Borough of Brooklyn, was inhabited and possessed by the chieftaincy of Canarsee, whose headquarters were at or near Canarsie, a name which still appears upon the City map.

The land occupied by natives was not always bounded by waterways, as is common among European communities, but they jointly occupied favorable places, and appear to have shown a neighborly feeling in allowing members of another clan to settle in their own home territory. We have reason to believe that the island of Manhattan was divided in ownership; the lower end of the Island being occupied by the Canarsee, while the upper part was controlled by part of the Weckquaesgeek of Dobbs Ferry, whose local Sachem was known as Rechewac. His headquarters were in Yorkville, at a village, of which all traces have been lost, situated somewhere about 94th Street and Park Avenue, Manhattan.

There was a native tradition to the effect that the land which was occupied by the Weckquaesgeek, a large tract that included part of the Bronx, all of Yonkers, and much of the western part of Westchester County as far north as Ossining, had once been inhabited by the Raritans, who had moved away and were settled along the valley of the Raritan River in Northeast New Jersey.

Both the Raritan and the Weckquaesgeek chieftaincies had such similar characteristics of aggressiveness and pugnacity that they seem to have come from similar stock. From this migration and transfer of territory we may learn something of the Indians' idea of the use of land, and of its abandonment if it proved inconvenient or if circumstances led them to find some other situation more desirable.

In this case it seems probable that a whole chieftaincy removed to another locality. Since the land which they thus abandoned was desirable for cultivation of the soil, it would seem that the motive for such a large migration must have been found in the lack of animal food, or what is still more likely, in some epidemic of disease.

Imaginative fears had a great effect on some of these superstitious people, who would leave their homes under such influence as was instanced by those who in 1660 occupying seven canoes loaded with women and children, fled from their home among the Minisink Lenape "for fear of a certain Manitto."*

---

* Colonial documents, Vol. XII, p. 315.

10

"SHANS-COMAC-AUKE"
AN INDIAN VILLAGE SITE
"THE ENCLOSED PLACE"

THIS IS A VILLAGE SITE OF THE CANARSEE INDIANS WHICH WAS
SITUATED ON THE WEST SIDE OF THE SHEET OF TIDAL WATER, KNOWN
IN LATER DAYS AS GERRITSEN BASIN. THE ANCIENT NAME, "THE EN-
CLOSED PLACE," MAY HAVE BEEN APPLIED IN INDIAN FASHION, BOTH
TO THE BASIN AND ITS CONTIGUOUS UPLAND. THE RYDER FARM ON
WHICH THIS STATION WAS SITUATED HAS YIELDED A LARGE NUMBER
OF STONE ARTIFACTS OF INDIAN CHARACTER, AND AT AVENUE U,
NEARBY, SKELETONS WERE DISTURBED WHICH WERE PROBABLY THOSE
OF INDIANS. THE BASIN WAS DAMMED BY GERRITSEN, AND A TIDE-MILL
WAS BUILT TO TAKE ADVANTAGE OF THE IMPOUNDED WATER WHICH
RAN OUT FROM THE BASIN AT LOW TIDE.

10a

WEIR CREEK BEACH AND VILLAGE
Bronx

THE SITE OF THIS ANCIENT INDIAN VILLAGE WAS EXPLORED BY THE LATE ALANSO
SKINNER, FOR THE MUSEUM OF THE AMERICAN INDIAN, HEYE FOUNDATION. IT IS SITUATE
ON THE SHORE OF EASTCHESTER BAY, AT THE MOUTH OF WEIR CREEK, AT THROGS NECI
IN THE BOROUGH OF THE BRONX. THE SHORE WAS LITTERED WITH INDIAN OBJECTS ANI
ON THE BANK THERE WERE A NUMBER OF FOOD PITS, FILLED WITH DISCARDED OYSTE
SHELLS, AND AN EXTENSIVE BED OF SHELLS AND WOOD ASHES. THE SITE IS DESCRIBED IN
PUBLICATION OF THE MUSEUM OF THE AMERICAN INDIAN. ITS SITUATION WAS IN TH
ANGLE OF THE INTERSECTION OF SCHLEY AVENUE WITH THE SOUTHWEST SIDE OF CLARENC
AVENUE.

THE SITE IS ONE OF THE MOST ANCIENT IN THE AREA OF THE CITY OF NEW YORI
ITS INDIAN NAME IS UNKNOWN.

10b

There are indications of the intermittent occupation of places and of the migratory customs of the natives of this region. They would occupy a favorable location at one season of the year, and make their way to another place where food or shelter were more readily secured at some other season.

The well-to-do and populous chieftaincy of the Matinecock, which occupied the northern part of Long Island from Flushing to Smithtown, were decimated by an epidemic of disease which they contracted after the white colonists had control of the surrounding country. In this situation the tribe was unable to migrate from its home and it was almost entirely wiped out by the progress of the disease.

Thus the Indian idea of the occupation of land was that each clan or chieftaincy, and each group of villagers, occupied and used the land on which they were settled so long as they found it desirable. They did not comprehend the European system of the ownership of land in fee, but seem to have regarded its occupation as a possession to which they were entitled, so long as they continued to utilize it. It is interesting to observe that a proposal has been quite recently advocated, as a means of meeting the difficulties of the American farmer, which "advocated nationalization of land by making use and occupancy the only title to land," which would be a revival of the Indian system.

Much of the mistrust and hostility which developed among the natives towards the colonists was due to this mutual misunderstanding as to the permanent ownership of land. The sales of land to which the natives agreed, proved to be to their disadvantage, sometimes their undoing. There were occasions, as in the case of the purchase of Staten Island, when a later generation bitterly demanded some consideration for the diversion of their homelands. And in certain transactions the unfortunate natives were quite unaware of the "deal" or sale, transacted sometimes by other Indians, in which they found themselves involved.

This situation applied to the eastern part of the Borough of the

11

Bronx. Natives of the Siwanoy chieftaincy occupied land abutting on the Sound from Norwalk to the Bronx river. In the year 1640 the Dutch authorities, in order to check the invasion of English settlers, entered into an agreement at Norwalk with chieftains of the Siwanoy, purporting to include the right of settlement from Norwalk as far East as Hellgate.

The hapless natives resident along this extensive stretch of territory, appear to have been unaware of the surrender of their rights, until white settlers arrived armed with a warrant issued by white authority to occupy their home-lands and their camping grounds. The effect of the dislodgement of the fishing population of the waters of the New York area, was to drive these people back into the forest, where their conditions of livelihood were radically changed, and it is assumable that much privation and hardship would have resulted. In the eastern part of the Bronx a large tract of land was thus awarded to John Throckmorton and his band of refugees from religious persecution in New England, who were accompanied by Mistress Anne Hutchinson and her family. The homes of these immigrants were raided and burned, their cattle and stock were killed, and the Hutchinson family was massacred by Indians, whose grievance against them was founded on the agreement made at Norwalk with natives perhaps unknown to them and for considerations of which they received no part.

We have found some stations that were evidently abandoned in great haste, such as that at 231st Street, in our present Kingsbridge, where a cooking vessel was found still standing in the ashes of a fire between the rocks, as it was left, perhaps steaming hot, by the poor native woman when called away in haste from her home.*

This occurrence may have taken place within historical times. We read of the natives around Nieuw Amsterdam, abandoning their homes in fear of the arrival of hostile Iroquois and crowding into other settlements near the City, only to be set upon by the armed

---

* This vessel is to be seen in the Museum of the American Indian, Heye Foundation.

12

train-bands of the Dutch, who slaughtered them without regard to their age, sex, or their friendliness to the white race. That dreadful outrage, which brought equally dreadful retribution, destroyed the confidence and friendship of the people who by right of occupation had for an unknown period dwelt in the area in which the great city has grown up.

III

THE NATIVES OF THE CITY

WE shall find several references in recorded history to the "Manhattans." There were no people so known, the natives so described were of other chieftaincies,* and were not known by the name of the Island, which first appeared in written form in the journal or log of Hudson's voyage of 1609. In that record Juet, the mate of Hudson's vessel, applied the name to the Jersey side of the river; in fact, he mentioned it as a place where there was a cliff or escarpment "the color of a white green" . . . "on that side of the river that is called Mannahata." This is supposed to have been Castle Hill, where a vein of serpentine rock is exposed and is visible from the river.†

An English map of 1610 places the name on the Jersey side of the Hudson River, though in this chart the New York side is also marked "Manhatin." Vingboom's map of 1639 located the "Manatuns" on the island. These explorers, map makers and the natives may not have understood each other very clearly.

Perhaps the natives misled the white men, by telling them the wrong name. They would regard this as good fun, for the Indian is a great practical joker.

The area of the present City of New York includes three hundred and eight square miles. Its boundaries may be studied on the map of the City and its five Boroughs are described in a later part

---

* The Archeological History of New York. Parker, 1920, Part II, p. 626.
† The Geology of New York City and Vicinity, Chester A. Reeds, 1930.

of this book. It occupies a unique and naturally advantageous position. Every one knows that the metropolis has grown up around the great water-ways which enter from the Atlantic Ocean to form the Outer Bay, the Narrows and the Inner Bay, and to fill the lordly Hudson River, which is an estuary of the sea, as well as the so-called East River, which is not a river, but a tidal link between the Bays and the Sound. These natural advantages were as desirable for the natives, as they have been for their successors.

Over these great water spaces natives possessing canoes could make their way from one locality to another. Life was fairly easy, food was plentiful, and communication between places and peoples was convenient. The natives prospered and increased.

Before the arrival of colonists from Europe there were within the area of the greater city not less than ninety-four stations, settlements and villages, on most of which the traces of occupation have been examined and investigated. These stations have been found in some cases to comprise a considerable number of lodges, as for instances, the village of "Snakapins" on Clauson Point, where about sixty food-pits were found, indicating that a similar number of lodges may have been in existence there. When De Vries visited the Indian station of Recquakie (or Rockaway) on Long Island, on the 24th day of March 1643, he counted thirty bark-huts in which from two hundred to three hundred inhabitants resided. This indicates that there may have been a proportion of seven persons to each hut, though Dankers and Sluyter tell of long bark-covered dwellings in which as many as fifty or sixty people made a home, each family having its own fire, and its exclusive vessels for use in cooking food. We may reasonably assume that there were several thousand natives resident in the area of the metropolis.

We learn little of the character, the manners and the appearance of these inhabitants from some of the ancient records. The white settlers of New Amsterdam regarded the race with prejudice and contempt. Their designation for the natives was "Willden," or Wild Men.

15

One of the earliest of these prejudiced records is contained in a book entitled "The New World," published in 1625 by De Laet, a Dutch historian. Unfortunately, like many of his people, he regarded the natives with disdain. He described them as "barbarians," and only briefly records their ways as follows:

"The Indians are indolent, and some, crafty and wicked, having slain several of our people. The Manhattans, a fierce nation, occupy the eastern bank of the river near its mouth. Though hostile to our people they have sold them the island or point of land which is separated from the Main by Hellegat, and there they have laid the foundations of a city called New Amsterdam."

"The barbarians are divided into many nations and languages, but differ little in manners. They dress in the skins of animals. Their food is maize, crushed fine and baked in cakes, with fish, birds, and wild game. Their weapons are bows and arrows, their boats are made from the trunks of trees hollowed out by fire."

"Some lead a wandering life, others live in bark houses, their furniture mainly mats and wooden dishes, stone hatchets, and stone pipes for smoking tobacco."

"They worship a being called Manetto, are governed by chiefs called Sagamos, are suspicious, timid, revengeful and fickle; but hospitable when well treated, ready to serve the white man for little compensation."

From this narration we should form the opinion that the natives of the district in and around the City of New York were shiftless and improvident. But upon examination of their habits and their living conditions we shall reach the conclusion that the necessities of their life precluded an indolent existence; and it seems that the author of "The New World" had been misled by the apparent idleness of some of the men in Indian villages who were probably huntsmen, bowmen or warriors resting and preparing themselves for another strenuous exercise of their craft.

It was doubtless the fact that our Indians of New York City were poor in worldly possessions. They seem to have been, for the most part, fisher-folk. We read in early local history of Indians visiting Pelham Bay in the summer time for the purpose of fishing. These were the Weckquaesgeek who lived on the upper end of the island of Manhattan, at Inwood. They had canoes of capacity suffi-

16

cient to carry the whole community to and fro. On one of their return journeys they were stopped by the inhabitants of Harlem, who were in fear of an Indian raid at that time, and their canoes were impounded. We may suppose that they had camped out during the fishing season on the shores of Pelham Bay and had shared in the capture of the numerous fish that were to be caught in the sheltered waters of Eastchester and Pelham Bays. They probably helped in accumulating those masses of discarded shells and the ashes of those fires which still exist along the shore lines of Pelham Bay and Eastchester Bay.

For them food was the main object of existence. Fish were very abundant and in the shallow places and the mud flats vast quantities of shellfish grew to an astonishing size. In the Hudson River the sturgeon and the shad swam, and along the Sound whales sometimes were stranded on the shore.

But such quarry, however plentiful, was not secured without considerable effort on the part of the natives. Canoes, nets, spears and fishing lines had to be made and kept in order; and there were always plenty of odd jobs for men to do in the making of household utensils, in carving the wooden dishes, in repairing the bark houses, in the slow shaping of stone axes, and in the flaking of new cutting edges on tools and weapons.

In the shell-heaps and in the food-pits of their villages, we have found large oyster shells usually packed at the lower levels, with smaller shells concentrated near the surface. We believe the pits were scraped out of the soil, and were lined with grass mats in order to provide a place in which to store dry foods, such as corn-cobs, beans and nuts . . . a sort of pantry. Then, when all the food in the store was consumed, the vacant pits were used as a deposit for rubbish. In them were dumped scraps of bone and vast accumulations of ashes and of the shells which lay around the village and perhaps cut the feet of the children.

Sometimes the pit was utilized as a grave in which to bury a dead Indian, or to place the remains of his pet dog. Some of them have been found to have had a snake or a turtle placed at the bottom of the pit, which probably was put there in some sort of ceremony, such as that of which Wassenaer tells in his old-time "Historiesch van Europa."

He says that they had a sort of sacrificial ceremony presided over by a "Devil-hunter." They would put some of their treasures into a kettle, and then put the kettle into a hole in the ground. They imagined that a terrible Horned Snake of which they were in constant fear, would crawl into the hole and would take possession of their offerings. When they next examined the pit, the kettle would be gone, so they supposed the Snake must have taken it. But undoubtedly the Devil-hunter went in the night and took it away himself.

IV

RELIGION

THE natives had developed a strong religious instinct, and had a system of belief which had a great influence on their lives. The breath of man was, in their view, his spirit.

A remarkable feature was a belief in life in a hereafter, and in the existence of a spiritual being, a "Great Spirit," superior to all others. Their idea of a heaven was very materialistic, for they imagined it to be situated in a southwest direction, and to have all kinds of material facilities. Hunting would be easy, and wild game abundant. In this place they supposed that they would live as they pleased, and would not have to work. It was a "happy hunting-ground."

It is not to be wondered at that they had a great fear of evil spirits, and, like many other peoples even in our days, considered that such evil spirits should be conciliated and in some cases, pro-pitiated by making sacrifices to them of goods or of animals.

To deal with the menace of these supposed evil spirits, a village sometimes maintained a "Shaman" or witch-doctor. His or her job was chiefly to concoct charms or to cast spells over those who were supposed to be affected or haunted by an evil spirit or by a ghost. Disease, to our Indians, presented two forms, either the presence in the body of the sick person, of some antipathetic object, or the temporary absence of the soul or spirit from its bodily residence. We may perhaps assume the two conceptions applied to cases of conscious illness or of unconsciousness.

19

In either case it was the purpose of the Shaman to aid the sick person either by the extraction of the adverse material assumed to be present in the body, by pulling it out, or by sucking it out, or, in a case of unconsciousness to pursue the errant spirit and cause it to return to the body. The Shaman probably had some crude knowledge of diseases and of remedies therefor, so sometimes he or she gained credit for the recovery of a sick person.

During sickness the natives were very attentive to the patient, but it is said that the sick person was often impatient to die if recovery was slow. We read that they were "extraordinarily charitable one to another."

The English poet, Pope, wrote of their religious beliefs:

> *"Lo, the poor Indian, whose untutored mind*
> *Sees God in clouds, or hears Him in the wind.*
> *To be, contents his natural desire,*
> *He asks no angel's wing, no seraph's fire."*

The details of the religious dogmas of our New York City natives were of little concern to their white successors. The Dutch took very little interest in them or their affairs, and spoke of their religion as mere devil-worship. The minister, Jonas Michaelius, writing to Holland in 1628, stated that he had hardly been able to discover a single good point in them.* He had never been able to master the Indian dialect, and regarded it as "a made-up childish language" and "entirely peculiar." His opinion, therefore, seems to have been arrived at without sufficient study, and certainly without any sympathy or interest. He spoke of the natives as being "uncivil and stupid as garden poles" . . . who "serve nobody but the devil, that is, the spirit which in their language they call Manetto."

The beliefs of a people are long lived, and vary little with the passage of a considerable period of time. The enquiries made by M. R. Harrington, veteran explorer and ethnologist, among the

---

*Year Book No. 17, Collegiate Reformed Protestant Dutch Church.

descendants of the Lenape, are recorded in the publications of the American Anthropologist* and afford a picture of their traditional beliefs and practices based thereon, which were inherited from their ancestors and were treasured by those of the same tribe who once occupied the site of New York.

Like all primeval peoples, the Lenape had developed simple but deep-seated beliefs, which influenced their lives and their doings and took the form of a religion. These beliefs were based, as are most forms of human imaginings, upon Fear—on the anticipation of invisible evils—on the prevalence of spirits, possibly malevolent— and on the dread of death. Such fears affect the minds, and color the lives of many peoples. To the Indian, the world in which he lived and labored was peopled with spirits, some good, some mischievous, some deliberately vicious. "The echo," says one old writer, "which resounds from the Cries of wild beasts in the night, they suppose to be the spirits of souls transmigrated into wicked Bodies." To evade their suspected malevolence the native would make great sacrifices, and to deceive and mislead these imagined persecutors, many devices were invented and various curious practices were followed. These conditions afforded, as most human beliefs do, a wide field for the unscrupulous practitioner and for the professional director. Thus the Shaman, the Medicine-man, and the Witch-doctor derived their living by encouraging the beliefs, the superstitions, and the fears of their followers and supporters.

But, superior to these imaginary inflictions, the Indian had conceived a greater authority in the form of a spirit more powerful than all the host that peopled the atmosphere, a Great Spirit occupying an indefinite space known as the Twelfth Heaven, in which place man received the objects for which he cared and for which in this life he had labored. These were to be afforded without effort on his part. The happy hunting ground was a place where the necessaries of existence were provided without stint or exertion.

---

* American Anthropologist, Vol. XV, No. 2, 1913.

This was the "happy-hunting ground," not far removed in its characteristic features from the Mahometan conception of paradise.

But as the Great Spirit, who is known to their descendants as "Gicelamu-Kaong," was supposed to be permanently settled in this highest realm of inert enjoyment, it was necessary to assume that any duties of a practical order for the benefit of mankind in which the Spirit might be concerned, would be delegated to less pre-occupied and stationary personages.

Harrington, by investigation among the descendants of our Indians, learned that the native conception in this regard was that several minor influences or spirits known as "Manitto," were occupied in regulating the operations of nature, in so far as they were assumed to affect the Indian race.

A Manitto, or manito may be taken to have meant the mysterious power of life.* As the white man assumed it, the word may have at times indicated either a good or a bad spirit, and by inference a god or a devil. The form of the term is probably Algonkian, for it appeared in the Massachusetts tongue as "Manitto" with the meaning "he is a god," and Roger Williams records the shortened form of "Manit" as "god."

A belief which was a fundamental feature of Indian concepts, was that of magic power, or a power superior to that of mankind which was inherent in the natural objects that surrounded them. This seems to have been the idea which was expressed in the word "Manitto," a magic or spiritual capacity which approached the attributes of a deity. If that magic power were directed towards the injury of man, the Manitto appeared to possess a malicious or devilish character, or if on the other hand the power attributed to a Manitto, were observed to be exercised beneficially to a tribe, a family or an individual, then the Manitto, thus clothed with the beneficial power, became worthy of recognition as a god.

It is thus probable that the term "Manitto," rather expressed the idea of a magic force, than of an individual spirit.

---

* Handbook of American Indians, 1911.

22

The enormous moral force of this idea controlled to a great extent the actions of the Indian. His life was absorbed in the desire to cultivate the good will of the benevolent magic force, and to ward off the hostile demonstration of evil influences. A variety of prescribed actions and ritual forms grew up around these beliefs, some taking the form of restrictions upon certain actions of the believer, prohibitions as to certain articles of food, taboos of certain classes or of actions and even of games played at certain defined seasons.

The early colonists, whose ministers, like Megapolensis, assumed that the Indian was limited in his belief to a single "Manitto," could have made little or no enquiry into the form or character of their beliefs; and had no appreciation of the extent or nature of their deep-seated religious system.

The "Manitto" which he described as their only object of worship, comprised, according to the description of their descendants, four spiritual beings, each of which had control of a fourth part of the terrestrial system, north, south, east and west, directing the winds and rains from each direction and acting as the helpers or delegates of the Great Spirit. The earth itself was regarded as the Mother of the race, providing as it did, the site of their homes, the food grown upon its bosom, and the wild forest which afforded cover for the coveted game.

These and other lesser spirits, even such as were believed to make animals and plants their habitation, controlled the minds and largely directed the doings of the Lenape.

The natives attached great importance to the mental vision or the dream, which to their minds indicated a contact with some of these spiritual beings with which the native imagination was filled, and by which their lives were surrounded. Those who had been favored with such manifestations of contact with the spirit world, were considered to be highly favored, and were sometimes regarded with special consideration. Their experiences were treasured by each individual and were memorized in the form of a story, a chant,

23

or an address, probably embellished by such imaginative trimmings as may have increased the interest, or added to the importance of their story.

Upon occasions of a meeting, of a pow-wow, or of a feast, the favored individual would be called upon, by the presiding officer or sachem, to relate his or her experience. The story would be closely followed by the audience, who would repeat the words of the raconteur, in which way some of these fantastic relations would become a part of the traditions of a village, or even of a tribe. An animal or other object connected with the vision, or one that had been the subject of a dream would assume a new character to the hearers, and its alleged intimacy with the dreamer would indicate that the people were being favored by some revelation from the spirit domiciled in the animal or object. An animal thus regarded would become connected with the people, who may then have adopted it as a mascot, an emblem, or a totem.

It was probably by this process that the various emblems, or "totems" of tribes, of chieftancies, and of village communities came into use, and the Turtle of the Unami may have been established in this manner as their insignia.

We may gather from these traditional beliefs and practices that the Lenape, and other Indian tribes, were very much occupied with spiritual matters, and were deeply imbued with what we may regard as superstitions.

Upon this foundation their social system, however crude it may have been, was based. Their methods of compensation for a wrong, their customs of marriage and of divorce, their education of the young, and their system of community ownership of property, were deeprooted in their social system and religious dogmas. If they had been studied with consideration and care by the European invaders, a better understanding might have been attained, and much of the frightful conflicts and brutal retaliations which disfigure our country's history might never have taken place .

By these considerations we may understand better than did De Laet, the race which he characterized as "Suspicious, timid, revengeful and fickle."

And perhaps we may be warranted in comparing their practices with those of their white successors in the Greater City and we may find that in some ways their rules of conduct, if adhered to, would put some of the selfish features of our system of civilization to shame.

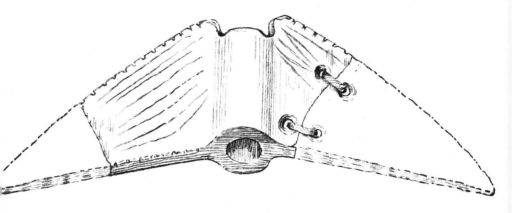

A CEREMONIAL STONE

THE CENTRAL PART OF THIS OBJECT WAS FOUND, WITH OTHER INDIAN ARTIFACTS IN THE VICINITY OF THE FARM DWELLING OF THE NAGEL FAMILY, WHICH STOOD AT 213TH STREET, ON THE BANK OF THE HARLEM RIVER. THE MATERIAL IS A YELLOW MARBLE WHICH DOES NOT EXIST IN NEW YORK CITY AND WAS THEREFORE BROUGHT TO MANHATTAN. THE OBJECT HAD BEEN BROKEN AT BOTH ENDS, BUT ONE FRACTURED END HAD TWO HOLES CAREFULLY BORED WHICH INDICATED THE USE OF THONGS TO UNITE THE FRACTURED PARTS. THE EDGES ARE NOTCHED, AND THE BOSS IS BORED. THE SURFACE IS SCRATCHED OR SCORED.

THE STONE APPEARS TO HAVE BEEN USED ORIGINALLY AS A CEREMONIAL OBJECT, MOUNTED ON A STICK AND CARRIED IN PROCESSIONS OR DANCES. PERHAPS THE NOTCHES ON THE EDGES MAY HAVE INDICATED THE NUMBER OF SUCH OCCASIONS.

FROM THE FACT THAT THE SCORINGS ON THE FACE BEGIN AND END ON THE MIDDLE PORTION, IT IS PROBABLE THAT THEY WERE MADE AFTER THE FRACTURED ENDS WERE LOST, AND THE CENTER PART MAY THUS HAVE BEEN IN USE AS AN AMULET OR ORNAMENT, HUNG ROUND THE NECK OF THE OWNER.

V
TRIBAL DIVISIONS

THE Lenape nation or "Delawares" as they were sometimes called, was composed of three divisions, the Unalaghtigo, the Unami, and the Minsi. Each division was identifiable by its "totem" or sign, of which that of our Unami was the Turtle. This sign is found to have been borne by clans residing along the Hudson River for some distance northwards, below the region which was occupied by the Iroquois and the Mohawks, which latter tribe had, rather appropriately, the totem of a wolf. In fact, the name Mohiks meant "wolf," and the members of the clan called themselves— Mohyks-ind—or "wolf-men," a description they fully deserved, for they are known to have been about as relentless and savage as the wild animal which constituted their emblem.

The Dutch immigrants soon found that their nearest Indian neighbors, the Canarsee of Kings County, were subject to the Iroquois confederacy, and were accustomed to pay Mohawk emissaries, usually a couple of old sachems who were sent for the purpose, an annual tribute or tax, which took the form of dried shellfish and of shell beads, probably the only goods they possessed.

When the tribute was not forthcoming, their overlords would send a band of armed men to raid the unfortunate tax-paying natives, burning their homes and their stores of food, and murdering men, women, and children without mercy.

There is no record of a direct conflict between the Iroquois natives and our Lenape, but it is probable that the former natives

26

had fought and conquered another race, the Susquehanna, who at some prior time had held the southern Lenape in subjection. Thus intimidated, the Unami of the New York City area submitted to the conquerors of their masters, and recognized their superiority by the payment of tribute.

The Unami Lenape embraced nearly all those chieftaincies which resided within the area of the present Greater City. In the Borough of the Bronx they shared part of the territory with the Siwanoy, members of a tribe which occupied lands extending along the Sound from as far East as Norwalk. Staten Island was divided in its occupancy between the Hackensack and the Raritan chieftaincies, but both were Lenape.

The Siwanoy were in occupation of some of Throg's Neck in the east part of the Borough of the Bronx, and the Weckquaesgeek of Manhattan were in the habit of residing there in the summer seasons. When the sale of that part of the City's area took place, the deed was executed by two Siwanoy Sachems and others, probably of the Weckquaesgeek.*

Thus several village sites in the east part of the Borough of the Bronx were shared with Siwanoy Indians, who were not Lenape, but were Mohegans, related to those New England tribes, which had come into contact and had engaged in severe conflict with the English colonists who settled in the district of the Massachusetts Bay, and overflowed into Rhode Island and into Connecticut.

Tribal inter-relationship also extended over a considerable number of the inhabitants of suburban territory such as those resident in the County of Westchester.

This situation was in existence at the time of the arrival of the white immigrants. The Dutch authorities took advantage of it, to deny to their Indian neighbors the possession of fire-arms, which they freely traded to the Iroquois, by which policy the unfortunate

_____

* The Archeological History of New York. Parker, Vol. II, p. 626.
Minutes of the Executive Council, Oct. 21, 1675.

Lenape found themselves inextricably bound to the condition of inferiority, and at the same time over-run by domineering white immigrants. But for this unfortunate combination the Lenape would probably, sooner or later, have fought it out with the Iroquois. A hundred years later a league was formed by the Lenape with other tribes for this purpose against the Iroquois, but the effort came too late.

VI
MARRIAGE CUSTOMS

WE may assume that the condition of the female among these primeval people was no better than is the situation of womankind in many backward communities of the present day. The woman was not regarded as the equal of the man, and was expected to perform all the household labor, besides the drudgery of farm work, and the bearing and care of children.

Young people married at what we should consider an immature age, a girl being considered to be in marriageable condition at fifteen years of age, and a young man at seventeen or eighteen.

A match was not particularly romantic. The girl was supposed to announce her willingness to become a bride by some adornment, such as a crown of shells or a mantle of feathers placed on her head.*

It is related that some young girls would wrap themselves in furs or finery and sit thus covered in the middle of the way, where a passing suitor or unattached bachelor might take notice of her. We observe the same practice with debutantes today. They also placed sometimes ornaments of shell-beads across the forehead, and wound round their necks a necklace, on the arm a bracelet, and sometimes they strung beads around their naked waists. In their hair they sometimes tied a stone ornament, made of a thin slab of stone or slate, in which two holes were bored.† These stones are

---

* De Laet, 1625.
† Skinner, Staten Island, Anthropological Papers, 1909.

sometimes styled by collectors, "amulets," and may have been regarded as tokens or bearers of good fortune. In either case they were doubtless highly prized.

A suitor being thus informed, decided upon and selected his mate, visited her home, and made a formal present to her parents. If the presents were accepted the parents consent was indicated, and the visitor walked off with his bride.

The marriage-tie does not seem to have been particularly binding, and the couple sometimes separated, the children then being taken by the woman.

Regarding the woman's duties in the household and the community, we may find that they were not unnecessarily onerous.

Work had to be done, and the division of necessary tasks between men and women was probably quite as much a matter of convenience or convention as are our household customs of today.

The woman controlled the home, and it is probable that she was regarded as the owner of the dwelling. The man had a definite share in the duties of domestic existence. He was regarded as the protector of the home, and was expected to be ready and to be in proper condition at all times to ward off enemies, to drive away wild beasts, to kill off rodents, to hunt for the supply of meat or to gather in fish food, to prepare the materials for trade, to undertake long journeys for that purpose, and to make and to maintain the weapons and tools he used, besides the simple implements which were used by the family. This division left to the woman the household tasks, which have been and still are to a great extent the accepted duties of womankind, and with the added work of cultivation of the field, her life was much the same as that of women in many other countries. Such habits and methods were crude, but were formed upon definite plans, and sometimes with a practical purpose.

The bearing and delivery of children, as with other peoples living under natural conditions, was relatively easy, not differing much from the ways of the wild creatures of the woodlands. Thus, upon the delivery of an infant, the mother, far from requiring a period of rest and recuperation, immediately resumed her task or occupation, and it is related that a prospective mother would burden herself with a bundle of sticks, which she carried around, as a method of strengthening her muscles for the anticipated carriage of the infant, which, swaddled to a board, would be hung by a strap from her forehead, and became her daily burden for a year following its birth. Their devotion to their infant children was conspicuous. The child received the greatest care and attention. Their songs were lullabies to their children.

It is hardly to be expected that these people would have been particular in the relations of the sexes, and they were not. But they certainly learned nothing in that particular from the rough and uncultured pioneers with whom they came in contact. The lot of women was not unnecessarily hard, but on the other hand, their habits and their moral conduct were practically unrestrained by any conventions.

Of their moral condition we have divergent accounts. Denton's information* would indicate that the women were loose in their relations with men, and that the marriage tie had little binding effect upon their conduct.

But other writers speak of the Indian women in different terms, mentioning their modesty and shyness.

Perhaps we may with justice arrive at the conclusion that each writer recorded the results of his personal observation, and that the experience of one may have been derived from the actions of a class of women wholly diverse from another. Or, in simpler terms, that the records of the doings of bad women differed from those of decent women, which lead similarly to very divergent conclusions today. The same discrepancies might apply equally to the male sex. The men were not all bad, neither were they all good. The women were not all immoral, nor were they all virtuous.

_____
* A Brief Description of New York. Denton, 1670.

We may also conclude that the natives of either sex gained little or nothing in the way of moral example from their contact with the rough manners and lustful appetites of many of the earliest arrivals from Europe.

GORGET FROM WESTCHESTER COUNTY, NEW YORK. THE GORGET, SOMETIMES KNOWN AS AN AMULET, WAS WORN AS AN ORNAMENT. *PHOTOGRAPH COURTESY OF THE MUSEUM OF THE AMERICAN INDIAN, HEYE FOUNDATION*

VII

OF INDIAN CHILDREN

IF we have little recorded fact regarding the personalities of the natives, it is natural that we should find less regarding their children. Certainly there must have been many of them in the villages and around the stations, and we may be sure that they played and enjoyed their young lives in their own way, in spite of the hardships and regardless of the poor circumstances into which they were born. All our American Indians have had some fixed practices, and one of them has always been to swaddle an infant on a board, and thus cause it to grow straight and upright. In this situation it did not lack attention or care, but was always close to its mother, while it hampered her actions very little. Children grew up inured to privation and used to stern control. They were trained to self control. One old writer says they were "as quiet as if they had neither spleen or lungs." Their voices were subdued and well controlled. Very young children were dipped into the cold water of a river to harden them, perhaps also to wash them.

The little ones played around much as other children do; they threw stones, fought each other and wrestled together. We have found fragments of tiny earthenware vessels, which may have been made for little girls to use in play at house-keeping. Some of the blunt arrow-points unearthed are possibly those with which little boys practiced shooting at a mark, at which they became very expert, a child of seven years of age being able to shoot a bird on the wing. It may be that some of the little stone blades we find

33

were toy knives with which they pretended to kill or scalp their imaginary enemies.

Children were taught to swim like ducks. The method was similar to an animal pawing its way through the water, cutting the liquid with the right shoulder. The children learned to catch fish with their hands by cautiously feeling under the stones where the fish hide. We may be sure that they were expert in hunting birds' nests.

They learned the ways of nature . . . they were taught to know the trees, the plants, the wild fruits, wild animals and their ways, birds and their habits, insects and their doings.

A boy was expected to learn the cry of wild creatures, to imitate the call of the wild turkey, the quack of the duck, and the honk of the goose. He had to be trained in the use of the various weapons of the chase, the dagger, the spear, the scalping knife, and to make and sharpen all the implements of which he made use. Besides this, the child had to learn the language, the beliefs and the social customs of the tribe. When a native was grown up, he had learned all these things, and had become astonishingly familiar with the details of nature. There is a story told of the amusement of some natives when a white settler admitted that he could not tell the difference between the patter of a dog's feet or the walk of a wolf, which the Indian easily recognized.

The domestic life of our natives probably included many of the games which have been found in use among their kindred and their descendants. Indoor amusements included guessing where an object was hidden under a row of mocassins, outdoor sports comprised a form of football, a game of skill in winter in which sticks were skidded over an icy or snowy surface, and trials of skill with bow and arrow, or competitions in throwing spears.

Another game was played with a number of small sticks, and a favorite gamble was played with fine small bones, which were colored partly black.

Outdoor sports included a sort of football on any level surface, while the boys and women looked on, sang songs and danced.

Some rattles were made of tortoise or turtle shells, of which one was found at Pelham Bay Park. These may have been for the amusement of babies or for use in ceremonies or dances. Our Indians seem to have been devoted to their children. In a child's grave at Tottenville there was a collection of objects which must have had considerable value to those who had lost the child. A child's skeleton at Throg's Neck was found under a mass of shells, but the head had been carefully protected between large stones, and above the grave a pottery vessel of most unusual form and beauty had been smashed to pieces, perhaps by the disconsolate mother.

Harrington found from these Indians' descendants, that the children inherited from their mother their nationality or membership in a clan or chieftaincy.

The boy became a member of an order or brotherhood by means of any vision or dream which would connect him in some way with the order.

Boys at a certain age were usually turned out of their homes to make their way through the wild woods, until they became somewhat used to woodland life. Then they were made to stay in the forest for several days entirely dependent upon their own exertions for food and shelter. In this situation it might be considered natural for a youth to spend some troubled nights, surrounded by the wild creatures who shared with him the place of his rest. And it was natural that his waking impressions or dreams took some form, or were connected with some creature or its doings.

Such a dream would constitute, upon his return to his home, a communication from the spirit domiciled in the object of the dream, granting to the boy a special relation to the subject of the dream, and enduing him with spiritual support throughout his future career.

Girls received less opportunities of that nature, and were accorded less consideration. Their instruction was concerned with the manifold duties of a household; they had to learn to cook, to clean skins, to prepare clothing, to do sewing, to care for the babies, and to carry on agricultural work.

An almost universal native practice consisted in the separation of women from their houses, and from association with others during a period of menstruation or at the birth of a child. On such occasions the female occupied and often constructed a small shack or hut, not too remote from her house, where she maintained her own existence. The mother was not welcomed in the dwelling for a few days after the child's birth.

SUB-IROQUOIS SHELL CUPS FROM THROGS NECK, NEW YORK CITY. *PHOTOGRAPH BY ALAN-SON SKINNER, 1917, AND COURTESY OF THE MUSEUM OF THE AMERICAN INDIAN, HEYE FOUNDATION*

VIII
LANGUAGE

THE Indian language in New England was first mastered and then reduced to written form by Roger Williams of Providence. The Lenape language has been examined and much of its form and character has been recorded by the missionary Heckewelder, and a list of words was gathered by Zeisberger, another missionary, who compiled from them a "Delaware dictionary." We are thus able to trace the meaning of many names of places in and around New York, which were in use by the Unami Lenape.

These records of their language show that it was quite similar to the speech of the natives in New Jersey and Pennsylvania who spoke the language of the Lenni Lenape, the "Men of Men." We must remember that it was not a written language, but was learned only by the ear. It is a very remarkable fact that the language had been so well learned by successive generations, that it had not become so distorted as to be impossible to understand. But we find that the dialect spoken by one of the tribes was not so much unlike other dialects, and that people of districts near one another could converse together. There were instances, however, where people living only forty miles apart were unable to understand each other's speech, possibly being members of different tribes, each having a dialect of its own.

This was of great importance to the natives because it enabled them to trade their native products with neighboring people.

Those Indian words which appear in the names of their homes and places are of particular value. Being recorded in written form in many conveyances of land in and about the city, it is possible to compare them with known words in the Lenape tongue. By this means we find that it is that language of which they were a part. Therefore we may conclude, in spite of the variations in those words due to the European law-writers who heard them spoken, that our natives of New York City were Lenape, and that the language they spoke and many of their fixed habits and methods were also those of the same tribe.

The Indian language included numerals. As in other systems, they seem to have been based upon the number of fingers on the two human hands. In this way it was very simple to reach the number ten, and then by adding a finger to each numeral to reach twenty. You can observe the persistence of the same simple method in our own system of figures, where we count above the ten fingers as four-ten, five-ten, six-ten, seven-ten, eight-ten, and nine-ten.

The Indian numerals of the Unami dialect were recorded by Heckewelder as:

N'Gutti	One
Nischa	Two
Nacha	Three
Newo	Four
Pal-enach	Five
Guttasch	Six
Nischasch	Seven
Chasch	Eight
Peschkonk	Nine
Tellen	Ten
Tellen-sac-n'gutti	Eleven (ten and one)
Tellen-sac-nischa	Twelve (ten and two)

and so on, up to "Nossinack," which was twenty.

38

Some Lenape words were preserved in a list which was written down in 1684, and is filed at Trenton, among the records of the State of New Jersey.*

THE SEASONS

Spring	Sickquan
Summer	Nippinge
Fall	Tacockque
Winter	Wean, or Ouean

THE ELEMENTS

Water	Ipis-Ipe
Snow	Whinne (the same word means "beautiful")

THE TIME

A day	Jucka
A week	Kisquenon
A month	Kisho
A year	Cothtingo

THE PLACE

Land	Auke, Akie, shortened to "Ock" and even to "K"
Meadow	Asqu
Bog or marsh	Assisku (Asgask is "green" and Asqu is a "meadow")
Pond	Paug
River	Seepe or Sipo (in which "ipe" is the water)

THEIR FOOD

Corn	Hosequen
Bread	Pone (we still use this word in Corn-pone)

---

* American Historical Record, Vol. I, 1873 and "Salem Surveys", pp. 64-68.

Meat	Iwse
Grapes	Virum—probably "Vivum"
Fish	Lamis
Salt	Seckha
Soup	Sac-sapaan

THEIR CLOTHING

Coat	Aquewan
Leggings or Stockings	Cockoon
Moccasins or Shoes	Seppock
Breeches	Soccutakan

THEIR IMPLEMENTS

Knife	Pocksucar, or Pachschican
Tobacco Pipe	Hopockan, or Hobokan
Axe	Tomahickan (which is still used as "tomahawk")
Hoe	Quippelens
Canoe, or Boat	Maholo, or Amochol
Dugout Canoe	Mushoon

ANIMALS

Hen	Tipaas
Chicken (a little hen)	Tipatit
Elk	Mides
Duck	Quing-Quing
Goose	Kahake
Turkey	Sickenom
Wild Cat	Lingwes
Wolf	Tukseat
Squirrel	Hamruk, or Hannick
Mink	Miningus, or Mininkus
Snake	Accoke, or Achgook
Beaver	Tomaque, or Yamaque
Fox	Hoccus
Fish	Lamiss

One peculiar feature of the Lenape language as spoken was that the sound of the letter "R" was absent. In this it resembled the Chinese who substitute for "R" the sound of "L." It would appear, from a study of our place-names, that the "R" which is seen in the writings of old deeds represented the sound of "OO" or "W." Thus we find the name of the Bronx written as "Ranaqua," which would be more correctly represented as "Wanaqua."

The native language had many subtle inflexions of meaning which made it very effective after it was learned, for instance:

Lenno—meant a man, or a male, and "L" in a word indicated that the subject of the word was male.

Ochquen—was a woman, or a female, and "Och" or "Que" conveyed the idea of the female sex.

Wuski-lenno—is a young male, or man, where the "lenno" reappears.

Ochquetit—is a young female, the "tit" indicates a little creature.

Pilawetit—is a boy baby, the "L" indicating the male sex, and the "tit" the small size of the baby.

Quetit—a girl baby, or "little woman," where "que" is the sign of the female sex and "tit" is the size.

In the same way "tipaas" is a hen and "tipatit" a chicken or little hen. The syllable "Que," which indicated a female, is the basis of the familiar term, "Squaw," which is widely applied to Indian women.

A very old man was "Mihilusis," in which the "L" has a place, and a very old woman was "Chochschisis," where "och" indicates the female and the "schisis" seems to have been a term of endearment or approval. "Schiki" was "pretty" or "nice."

When they spoke of animals they described them as "he" or "she" beasts, such as "lenno lingwes" or as we might say, "Tom Wild Cat," and "Ochque lingwes," "Pussy Wild Cat." But sometimes a male or female beast had a name of its own, and a she-bear was "Nauscheach," while a male-bear was "Konoh."

When we examine the Indian names of places, we shall find that the natives were minutely observant of natural features, and we may learn much of the characteristics of a place by the Indian name. A place-name nearly always ended in the word, "auke," literally "land," but by inference meaning a "place." So any Indian name which ends in some form of this word can be readily traced to an aboriginal origin. Europeans wrote it down as "ock," "ok," "ick," "ik," "auk," and even as "ac." It has the meaning of our words "the place where" or "where there is."

The language had many inferential meanings. Our local Indians had a habit of prefixing the letter "N" to a spoken word, which puzzled many writers, but is easily explicable. It was the "N" from "Lenni," the sign of the male, and by inference it conveyed the idea of ownership of the subject of the spoken word. In the same way "Matta" meant "No," but it was frequently clipped to "M."

Following are the principal Lenape words used in making names of places:

ACKI—HACKI. Variations of "AUKE" (see below). "The earth."

AKIE—INK. Earth, place (see AUKE).

APPAQUI—APPOQUI—APPUHQU—composed of "APPO" and "AUKE." "Covered ground," thus, "covering" or "roofing" or "thatching of a lodge." By inference, the reeds, flags or rushes composing a roof, such as the cat-tail flag or typha patifolia.

APPO—APPA—Sometimes clipped to "AP." "To cover, shaded,," and by inference a "roof-covering," sometimes implying a "trap."

ASQU. Grass, or a meadow or marshy tract on which green reeds or grasses grew.

ASGASK. The color, Green.

ASHAUE or ASSAWA, sometimes clipped to "SHAH," "in the middle," indicating a midway place or location.

ASHIM. Appears as "HASHIM;" "A spring of water."

ASSIN—ASSINI, sometimes clipped to "SIN," "Stone," and by inference any hard material such as iron or brass, hard or stone-like in character, reminding us that the native had no knowledge of metals.

ASSISKU. Marshy, miry, muddy, boggy ground, probably a compound of "ASGASK—ASQU" clipped to "AS—AS—QU."

AUKE—AKIE shortened to "OCK," "OGUE" or "OK," "INK" and even to the letter "K," appears also as "ACKI," sometimes written as "HACKI." The ground, land, earth, thus a situation, a place, or locality, usually used as the last syllable of a place-name. Thus indicating the locality-character of a word. It may perhaps be understood as "The place where."

AWOSS. "Beyond," by inference, "On the otherside."

ES—IS. "At," or "Near."

HAKINK. "In or on the earth."

HITOCK. A tree.

ING—INK—ICK—UNK, ENK, all derived from "AUKE." A locative, very much used, denoting a place or locality (not to be confused with "UCK"). Indicating, "the place where" (see AUKE).

IPE—IPIS and dropping the first syllable applied as "PE." The use of "N" (which see) as a prefix may cause it to appear as "N'IPPI." "Water"—"Watery." It appears as a suffix "PE," or added as an adjective, "PE—AUKE," "Water land" or "marsh." Turnbull gives in Connecticut, "NIPPI," "water"—"Nippiog," "Waters"—"Nippeash," "waters."

ITTUK. A river, or flowing water, or a stream of water.

KAU. "Sharp" or "Pointed."

KETAN—KITTAHIKAN. Shortened to "HIKAN" in compound words. The sea or the ocean. The word conveys the idea of a sawing or cutting tool, probably in reference to the intermittent motion of the ocean tides ebbing and flowing back and forth.

KIKHICAN. A boundary (Zeisberger), possibly a water-boundary or the sea-shore, as "HIKAN" is the "ocean."

KIT. Large, or wide.

MATTA. Bad, evil, or ill. By inference negative, and so used as the word "NO." Sometimes clipped to "M," as "M'bi or "M'pi," "Bad water."

N. Widely used as a prefix to any words, not commencing with "N." Derived probably from "LENNI," a "Man" or "the Man," and by implication meaning "I." Thus, "NEPE" meant "I also." Sometimes used before vowels, as "N'IPPI"—"Water," indicating ownership of the water supply.

OCQUE—WEQUA—UCQUE. Found also as "QUA" or "QUE" and in the corrupted form of "ONGK." "Beyond," "as far as," "at the end of." By implication, "bounded place," indicating a "limit," or a line marking the bounds of a tract of land.

OMPSK. A rock.

PASAECK. A valley.

PAUG. A pond or water hole, perhaps composed of "PE" and "UCK," indicating a "water-place."

POQUA or PAUQUE. "Clear or open," when applied to land which is cultivated or cleared, that is, freed of timber. Turnbull explains a variation in use in Connecticut, where "Poquannoc," indicates land naturally open. "Pauque-Auke" is land which has been made clear, or cleared from timber; and "Pauquettah-hun-auke," conveys the idea of land that has been dug over, plowed, or broken up, and is under cultivation.

QUANON—QUONNE—QUINNE. Long, lengthy.

QUENEK. Length.

QUEQUAN. Trembling or moving.

SAC—SAKI. "The mouth of a river," or "outlet" of a lake or pond. Used also to indicate "soup" as "SAC-sapaan." Perhaps indicating the open mouth of the vessel in which the corn soup was contained.

SCHIKI. Pretty or nice.

SEEPE—SEEPO—SEAN—SIPPO. A river.

SIPUNK. To, or into, the River, derived from "SIPO."

SCHAGASKET—compound of "SCHAG—ASKEET." "Wet grass," implying marsh grass or bog, since "ASGASK" is Green color.

SUKSIT. The color "Black."

TACHAN. "Wood," "timber."

TATA. "Shaking" or "waving."

TIC—TUC—TUCK—ITTUK. "A creek," or "moving water," applied to ebb and flow of tides.

TUKQU, by dialectical habit found in Connecticut as "P'TUKQU." "Round" or "circular."

UT, ET. "At," "near," "nearby."

WAPIM. "A chestnut."

WAMPMIS. "Chestnut tree."

WAMPIM—INISI. A chestnut tree with reference to its trunk. The fruit or flower of such a tree would have its own descriptive name.

WAPSU—WOAPSU—WOAPEN—WAP—WAMP. White, also applied to indicate brilliancy such as "WOAP—SUM," literally "white-light," thus indicating sunshine.

WEQUA—WEHQUE—WIQUA (see OCQUE). As far as, or at the boundary or limit. These variations are seemingly due to the effort of "European scribes to record the sound of "OU—AY."

WIK—WIG. "A house," whence the common term for an Indian house, "Wigwam."

WINNE. "Fine" or "beautiful," applied as "WHINNE," to indicate "snow."

WOM. "Going," or by inference, "movement" or "motion."

IX

INDIAN NAMES OF PLACES

THERE are Indian names of places, some of which are still in use around the Greater City, each of which gives a little picture of the locality as it was in Indian days. In Jersey we find such native names as Passaic, Peapack, Teaneck, Communipaw, Hackensack, and others.

In Westchester County we have Chappaqua, Sing Sing, Mamaroneck, and many more.*

In Long Island there are many still in use, such as Patchogue, and others changed in form such as Rockaway, Maspeth, and Jamaica.†

In Brooklyn we still use the name Canarsie, by which the natives of Kings County were known. The name indicates "a place fenced in," perhaps indicative of the physical situation of Kings County, nearly surrounded or fenced in by the ocean.

Armbruster finds in its earlier form of "Canaarsee" a reference to "Konoh," the bear, which might have been the totem of the chieftaincy.‡ Around that settlement there were extensive "planting grounds" fenced to keep out the deer. Gowanus is another native name still applied to a bay and to a canal in West Brooklyn. It is composed of two Delaware words—"gauwin," to sleep and "es," little, or "sleep little," which Tooker considers may have

---

* "Aboriginal Westchester", Vol. IX. Westchester County Historical Society, 1932.
† "The Indian Place Names on Long Island." W. W. Tooker.
‡ Coney Island." Eugene L. Armbruster, New York, 1924.

been the name of a native known as "Gouwane" who lived nearby in early colonial days. But it more probably represented the Indian idea of the secluded little bay, or of the inlet which now is the canal.

In Queens we have Rockaway, the Indian "Rechouw-akie," or "Place of Sands." There are other names of Indian origin still in use on Long Island, such as "Jameco," modern Jamaica, which was applied to a beaver-pond near an Indian settlement at Jamaica.

Maspeth is an English form of the Indian name "Maspaetches" which was applied by the natives to the swamp lands along the Newtown creek, and was made up of syllables cut out of several native words. "Mecht-pe-es-it," or "at the bad water place," is a description of the one-time stagnant swamps of that part of Queens County.

In the Bronx we have in use today the word "Mosholu," applied to a brook in Van Cortlandt Park, a name which is not easily dissected. It is probably a contraction from a longer word containing some reference to "Musquetany," a place of reeds or rushes, whence is derived the name of our nationally-detested insect, the mosquito.

We still have Manhattan, "Minna-atn," the "Island of Hills," or as we would say, "Hill Island."

Croton is a name in common use, because it was applied to our water system, upon which the City grew up. The name is Indian, and it is still in use in the City, applied to Crotona Park, Morrisania, in the Borough of the Bronx.

The Croton River ran across the County of Westchester between the chieftaincies of the "Sint Sinck" and the "Kitchawonk." The stream has been used to make the great reservoirs of the Croton system, from the high level of which the water gravitates to the great city. The Indian word as the Europeans wrote it, appeared as "Ki-wigh-tig-nock" which was clipped to "Qua-tuck-on," or "Qua-tu-on," and now is Croton. Its meaning is "the boundary stream place," or as we should say, "the stream which forms the boundary."

Some of the native names of their home sites and of the lands on which the white settlers made their homes, have been preserved in ancient documents. These names were compounded of several words, which described some prominent natural feature of the place.

The Indians were accustomed, in making a compound word to clip other words to a syllable, sometimes even to a letter or two, but each of these parts of the compounded word described something of the character of the place.

Most of these names have disappeared from City records, which is rather a pity, since they were more interesting and often more descriptive than their European substitutes.

So we have Brooklyn in place of "Menachawik," meaning "The home fenced in." We have Queens County instead of "Rechquaakie," "the place of sands."

The "Bronx" is neither so correct nor pleasant a name as "Wanaqua," the end place or peninsula, as we should say.

Yonkers does not sound so agreeable as "Neperhan," "Ni-ipi-an," the "place where there is land between the waters."

Inwood is not so descriptive as "Shora-kap-ok," nor is Spuyten Duyvil any improvement on the name "Paparinemin," the "making-a-false-start-place," the place where the tides used to ebb and flow twice as often as elsewhere.

These Indian names often tell us something of the features of a place which may have disappeared long ago.

We have in the Borough of Queens an inlet from the Sound which we call Cow Bay. It gets its name, not from a domestic animal, but from the Indian word "Kowe," which is a pine tree. Its shores were probably covered with such trees in past days.

The great estuary of the Hudson, in which the tides move back and forth daily, was known among the natives as "Mahikanituk," which is a compound of three words:

Massa, "great"—clipped to "Ma"
Hikan "ocean"—the chief feature of which was
its ebbing and flowing tide
Ittuk "river"

Thus conveying the idea of the "Great Ocean-like River," or a Great River of Ebb and Flow," showing us how the Indians observed natural features, and how in this case they noted the motion of the tides in the Hudson, which is for a part of its course a tidal estuary.

In the suburban districts around the Greater City, many Indian names are still in use. Some tribal names are preserved in Raritan, Tappan, Haverstraw (Haverstroh), and in New Jersey a number of places such as Pamrapo, Communipaw, Hoboken, Passaic, Watsessing, Hackensack, Teaneck, and others.

In nearby Westchester County we still use some Indian names of places, such as Katonah, Armonk, Chappaqua, Ossining, Croton, Mamaroneck, Manursing, Nepperhan, and Tuckahoe.

On Long Island, besides those already named, we shall find Manhasset, Montauk, Merrick, Massapequa, Quogue, Shinnecock, and quite a number of others.*

These names are now the only obvious evidences of the one-time Indian ownership of the Greater City. Their village sites and their fishing and hunting stations are nearly all covered with modern streets and buildings, their pathways are buried below our paved streets, their marks upon the deeds by which they traded away their inheritance of the land are hidden in documents filed away at Albany, and the objects which they cast away or lost around the sites of their humble homes have been recovered by patient exploration and are often the only physical proof of aboriginal occupancy.

In a succeeding chapter will be found some of the Lenape names of places, which are recorded in the history of the City of New

* "The Indian Place Names on Long Island." W. W. Tooker, New York, 1911.

York, and these may lead others to take an interest in unscrambling some local native name that may be still in use, or which may be recorded in some ancient document.

1654 — THE PELL TREATY OAK — 1906

PELHAM BAY PARK

THIS WAS THE ANCIENT TREE, UNDER THE ONCE SPREADING BRANCHES OF WHICH THOMAS PELL MADE THE AGREEMENT, IN 1654, WITH THE SACHEMS MAMINIPOE AND WAMPAGE, BY WHICH THEY CONVEYED TO HIM THE VAST MANORIAL ESTATE OF NINE THOUSAND ACRES IN PELHAM AND NEW ROCHELLE. THE TREE WAS SITUATED IN FRONT OF A NATIVE VILLAGE OF THE SIWANOY CHIEFTAINCY, THE SITE OF WHICH IS ON THE ELEVA- TION DUE NORTH OF THE TREE. IT WAS EXPLORED FOR THE MUSEUM OF THE AMERICAN INDIAN HEYE FOUNDATION BY THE REV. WILLIAM BLACKIE, WHO FOUND "ABOUT TWENTY FOOD PITS FILLED WITH SHELLS, AND THE GRAVE OF A DOG." RECENT EXPLORATION BY THE FIELD EXPLORATION COMMITTEE OF THE NEW YORK HISTORICAL SOCIETY HAS TRACED THE INDIAN SETTLEMENT EASTWARD TO THE SHORE OF THE SOUND.

50

X

INDIAN NAMES OF SOME PLACES IN THE CITY OF NEW YORK

In deciphering the meaning of Indian Place-names, which is a most interesting pursuit, several points should be borne in mind:

The Indian designation of a place usually described some significant feature, which was most important to the native mind.

Indian names of places were compounded of several words, but were clipped into syllables that would run together.

Indian words were not in writing, but were transformed into the corresponding sounds of European tongues by the law-clerk who inscribed the documents in which they appear in written form.

Variations in the Indian words in their written form were due to local dialects, or to the personal pronunciation of the native who informed the clerk. Some variations may be due to an Indian deliberate mispronunciation by way of a joke.

The name of a place is not to be attributed to some person who resided there, because the person would remove to some other place upon sufficient cause or would die. It is more probable that a person would adopt the name of a place than that the place would adopt his name, which was usually a mere fanciful appellation. With these considerations in mind, we proceed to examine the meaning of some of those places which are recorded in the history of the City of New York.

KAPSEE

The extreme southerly end of Manhattan Island, which name was applied to the rocks in the tide-way, now buried under Battery Park. There was a landing place at Pearl Street, where the shore was liberally covered with shells, and natives probably spent a good deal of time on the shore as they came from or went to Brooklyn, but there does not seem to have been a settlement in the locality. The land was rocky, there was no near-by drinking water, and the place was very exposed. We may imagine the ridicule with which the natives would regard white people who had selected such an undesirable place for a settlement. The name seems to have been compounded out of several words:

"KAU—OMPSK—IC," "KAU—P—SI" or "KAPSEE." "Where there are sharp rocks," or "The sharp rock place."

WERPOES

This was a site near the Collect (Kalch) Pond, or rather ponds, which occupied the low ground around the Tombs Prison. There was an Indian site on Pearl Street, which was liberally covered with shells, an unfailing sign of native occupancy. This was destroyed in the course of early street opening and subsequent buildings and was not explored. The Indian name of the place is preserved in a document in which reference is made to the place called "Warpoes," which was applied to a space of cultivated land north of the ponds. The name "Werpoes" seemed to Tooker to have been derived from the Delaware word "Wipochk," meaning "a bushy place;" probably in its original condition the village may have been surrounded with thickets and brambles.

RECHTAUK

This was a settlement of natives which became famous (or infamous) as the scene of the dreadful slaughter of Indians by the Dutch soldiery in 1643.

The letter "R" is a European equivalent for a Delaware sound. The name was written as "N'aghtonck" by Schoolcraft. The "R" or "N" were probably the nearest equivalent to the queer sound emitted by the natives which was sometimes regarded as "R" and sometimes as "W" or "L." The word is compounded of "Reckqua" or "L'eckwa," meaning "Sand," and "Auke" the familiar locative. It describes as "The Sand Place" the nature of the village site on Corlears Hook which was probably situated at or near Jefferson and Henry Streets.

SAPOHANIKAN

Sometimes written "Sappokanikan," probably by error. This was a cultivated area on the shore of the Hudson, at Gansevoort Street, which does not appear to have been a settlement, for there was no fresh water supply near by. It was probably a landing-place for canoes proceeding to and from Hoboken, the "place of tobacco-pipes."

"Sappo" meant Tobacco, and "Hanikan," a Plantation, and thus the place was known as "The Tobacco Plantation."

SHEPMOES

This site, which was never explored, is mentioned in a document of the Dutch period. Its situation was evidently just south of the farm of Pieter Stuyvesant, probably at East 13th Street, where there existed in ancient times a little island of cultivable ground rising from the salt marsh bordering the East River. Round this island a little fresh-water brook made its way. The Mutual Gas Company's plant is now situated at this place.

The name gives us a dim picture of the site, for it is composed of "Sepunk," meaning "to or into the river," otherwise a brook or stream, and "es," a little thing, whence Shepmoes gives us "The little brook into the river," descriptive of the small fresh-water brooklet which once found its way into the East River in the midst of the wide-spreading salt-marshes.

SHORAKAPPOK

The native settlement on the extreme north end of the Island of Manhattan, located in or near Inwood Hill Park. The area known most definitely to have been so occupied was a village site extending along Seaman Avenue, and there was a station in the wild woods of the Park extending around the interesting Indian cave, with lodges situated close to Spuyten Duyvil Creek. The name survives in deeds and charters relating to the locality, while it also appears as the name of that part of Spuyten Duyvil Creek which connects with the Hudson. Such an application of a name to both land and contiguous water is characteristic of Indian nomenclature, but there must have been some feature of both that befitted the use of the same name. The name has afforded a good deal of speculation, and has brought out several definitions, such as "The sitting-down place, which does not appear to apply to the stream, and "Wet-ground place," which does not describe the most important feature of sheltered woods and winding waterway. It seems that these are best met by the application of well-known Lenape words:

"N'ashaue—kuppi—ok," the closed-between place, descriptive of both the land and of the winding water-course shut in between the hills of Inwood and Spuyten Duyvil.

RECHEWANIS

This was a native settlement which was sold at a late date, and by the record of the transfer it appears to have been situated in the vicinity of 94th Street and Park Avenue, near which there was a little brook, fed by a spring. It was the home of the Sachem Rechewac, whose people resided in Washington Heights and in the Bronx. The chief adopted the name of his home, which described

"The place near the sands"

overlooking the shores of Hellgate Bay and the sandy point that

54

then extended along the mouth of Harlem Creek into the East River.

RANACHQUA

More probably "Wanachqua," the native name of the tract in Morrisania which Jonas Bronck acquired from the resident natives. Around the Morris house, which was near the site of Bronck's colonial home, we found some fine specimens of native tools, and in front of the old building there was a shell-pit under the lawn which had never been disturbed.

"Wanachquiwi—auke," clipped to "Wanachqua," meant, "The end-place" which describes the peninsula forming the termination of the mainland where it met the waters of the East River and Harlem River.

QUINNAHUNG

Now known as Hunt's Point, and given over to a wilderness of city rubbish and ashes, and a huge gas-making plant. At the foot of the property of the late Charles Dickey, there were deposits of shells. Near the little burying-ground, made notable as the last resting-place of Drake, there was the site of the old Richardson dwelling, and nearby many shells gave indications of Indian existence at and around the spring which provided the water used in the farm dwelling.

South of the cemetery a gravel pit had been opened, and there W. L. Calver found a real treasure buried about two feet down in the gravel. It was a roughly-formed celt, a prehistoric hand tool, the earliest form of implement made and used by man. It indicated a very ancient occupation of this promontory by prehistoric human beings.

At Hunt's Point there were shell beds indicative of fishing camps. The Indian name for Hunts Point was "Quinnahung." Quinne is "long," and Ongh is "beyond," as if they were pointing to the lengthy neck and saying "The long-beyond," or as we should more prosaically say, "The long point."

SNAKAPINS

This was an Indian village, the name of which was recorded. It was situated on Cornell's Neck, which is now known as Clauson Point. Traces of native occupation were observed by W. L. Calver, upon the widening of the east side of Sound View Avenue at its intersection with Leland Avenue. The site was then carefully explored by Alanson Skinner and this author. The situation of many pits was measured and plotted on a plan. One interesting discovery was the skeleton of a full-grown man buried beneath the ashes of a large fire situated about the center of the village. The remains were uncovered by Amos One-Road, a native American Indian, then employed by the Museum of the American Indian, Heye Foundation.*

The Indian name of this village has been regarded as having the meaning of a "Ground-nut," but as there is no probability that nuts existed there, nor that its population would have been particularly interested in such a humble object, we may take the liberty of discarding the suggestion and of applying a reasonable explanation, better descriptive of the locality. The village was situated on a promontory extending between the waters of Pugsley's Creek and those of the East River. The termination seems to be some mispronunciation of the locative "ING," and the name seems to have been compounded out of the words

"SEAN—AUKE—PE—ING"

"River-Land-Water-Place," thus conveying the idea of a "place where the land is between river and water," which is precisely its physical situation.

The meanings of a number of localities in Brooklyn and Queens were carefully studied and explained by the late Rev. W. W. Tooker, and may be found quite fully set forth, in his book, "Indian Place-names on Long Island," New York, 1911.

---

* See Publications of the Museum of the American Indian, Heye Foundation, 1919.

XI
PERSONAL NAMES

INDIAN personal names are very difficult. In his or her baby-hood the child was given some pet name which lasted until it grew up. Then he or she adopted a different name, sometimes derived from a dream, or sometimes from some incident that had occurred, or even some fancied resemblance of the person to an object. Nick names were frequently applied.

If a boy distinguished himself by some deed of skill or valor, he might take a name that would remind people of his prowess. These names, when they were spoken to a Dutch writer, frequently became distorted and unpronounceable.

In a long list of personal names which appear upon deeds for the purchase and sale of land, we find few that we can comprehend. Some of them seem to have been names of places from which the native came, some are imaginative, and others are to us mere jumbles of sounds.

So we find the chief known as Gouwane, living near Gowanus Creek, in Brooklyn. He was probably known by the name of the locality, which is "Sleep-Little," or the name may have been his own, indicating his watchful character, the "Wakeful-one." On the whole it seems more likely that a person would become known by the name of the place, rather than that the place would be known by his name, which applied only to him and would die with him.

Sometimes the Dutch lawyers got very much mixed over a

personal name, as for instance, that of the chief sachem of Rye, whose name appears in various deeds as:

Shonarock
Shonearockite
Shanarockwell
Janorockete
Shuwannorocet

or his half-brother

Romacqua
Rawmaquaie
Ramacq
Ramakque
Roksohtohkor

The worst of all is "Awoejhackias," which was written as the name of a Westchester native as late as in 1782.

XII
TIME

THE Indians of New York City had no other timepiece than the rising and setting sun to mark the passage of a day, and the moon's variations which marked the progress of time in the duration of a month. The passage of time was thus reckoned by observation of the sun and the moon. The year told its own story.

The Lenape and probably other Indians, divided the year into the four changing seasons; upon which we, with all our acquired knowledge, cannot improve.

The short days of winter, the return of spring, the heat of the summer, and the hoped-for harvest season, were recurrent events, but meant to them only a repetition of circumstances to which they looked forward, or more readily forgot.

As to lesser periods than the day, they seem to have had no knowledge, nor had they perhaps any need for such precise measurement. On the extent of their own age they were very indefinite, for they had no record other than mental recollection. Heckewelder found that for the most part they computed their ages not from birth, but by the seasons that had passed since some remarkable event had occurred within their own recollection.

On some of the stone objects, such as those of a ceremonial character which have been found in and near the City, there were scratches or nicks which seem to have been "tally marks," and seem to have recorded the recurrence of events in the life of the owner of the object.

Old age seems to have been respected, and experience and wisdom were expected to exist in a Sachem, as they should in our legislators and rulers of today.

FLAKING ARROWHEAD WITH BONE TOOL
N. Y. STATE MUSEUM, 1920

FLAKING STONE POINTS

THE PROCESS OF MAKING A STONE POINT REQUIRED CONSIDER-ABLE PRACTICE. THE ROUGH BLANK WAS FIRST KNOCKED INTO SHAPE OUT OF A PEBBLE, OR A SLAB OF FLINT, OR A SIMILAR HARD STONE. THEN THE BLANK WAS SHAPED BY USING A BONE TOOL, SUCH AS A PIECE OF HORN, OR A BEAR'S TOOTH, HELD IN ONE HAND, PRESSED HARD AGAINST ANY PROJECTION ON THE BLANK, AND WITH A STRONG JERK, A FLAKE WAS THROWN OFF. IN THIS WAY A CUTTING EDGE WAS GRADUALLY FORMED AND THE BLANK WAS SHAPED INTO ONE OR OTHER FORM, TO BE UTILIZED AS A KNIFE, A DAGGER, A SCRAPER, OR AN ARROW.

A SMALL POINT COULD BE MADE BY A PRACTICED HAND IN ABOUT HALF AN HOUR.

FOR MAKING LARGE BLADES, THE TOOL OR TOOTH WAS SOME-TIMES MOUNTED IN A STICK, WHICH RESTED AGAINST THE SHOULDER.

XIII
PATHWAYS

THE paths trodden through the country by Indians were in many places the predecessors of our modern highways.

In "Indian Paths in the Great Metropolis,"* the course of a number of known pathways within the area of the City was traced, and these were found to have usually extended from one Indian station or village to another. Hence it may be inferred that the various villages, or settlements, were connected to others by trails, which served the very useful purpose of conveying food and supplies from one locality to another, and also helped to keep the people acquainted with each other, by visits and by messages. Some of these paths must have been in existence for a very long time. We find that a path in Kings County, which ran from a very important station at Flatlands to another at New Utrecht, was known as "Mechawanienk," "Mechawa" meaning ancient, "ani" meaning a pathway and "enk" a place. This "Ancient Pathway" is described by its Indian name in a conveyance of land written as early as 1652. It was widened by settlers of Flatlands into a "Wagon Path," in 1682, and by 1704, it became known as "Kings Highway," which name it still continues to bear.

There was another known and probably very ancient path which extended from the lower end of Manhattan up the entire length of the island to Kingsbridge, and there connected with the long trail to the Mohawk region. The path was known as "the Weck-

---

* Published by the Museum of the American Indian, Heye Foundation.

quaes-geek Path," which became The Bowery, thence it followed the course of the old Bloomingdale Road from Fourteenth to Twenty-third Streets, and thence ran irregularly up the island and became known as the Boston Post Road. After it reached Harlem (where it was easy to ferry over to Morrisania), it proceeded as St. Nicholas Avenue now runs to 168th Street, and by the course of the old Kingsbridge Road which is now Broadway, to Kingsbridge. There the path led to the "Wading Place," which was a shallow part of the Spuyten Duyvil Creek, where one could wade across at low tide and so leave the island of Manhattan.

On landing, you proceeded up Broadway to 231st Street, where you turned abruptly east, passing over the marshy course of a little brook that ran into the Harlem River, and on scrambling up the bank on the other side, you arrived in Kingsbridge.

Here you found another Indian path which ran right and left. The left was the trail to the Mohawk region, along the line of the Albany Post Road northward up the east side of the Hudson. To the right the path turned and was known as "Sack-er-ah," from "Schaik-ahik," the Sea-shore, and "Ani," a path, or the "Shore Path," which led, by way of the Old Boston Post Road, across the Bronx River at Williamsbridge, and close to the boundary of Mount Vernon to Eastchester, thence to Pelham, New Rochelle, and along the approximate course of our modern Boston Post Road through Mamaroneck, Rye and Portchester, to the homelands of the Connecticut and Massachusetts tribes.

Another important trail on the New Jersey side of the bay was known as "The Indian Path to Minisink," by which our Unami Lenape communicated with their relatives, the Minsi.

When all these known paths, and others that must have led to and from Indian villages, are placed upon our City Map, it appears that the main paths on Long Island connected together and led to Brooklyn, converging at a point opposite the southern end of the island of Manhattan.

On the island at Pearl Street, there were scattered so many oyster shells that the shore was white with them, and hence the Dutch settlers gave to a street, which they laid out along the shore, the name of Pearl Street. It is evident that many canoes must have landed there in Indian days and that the natives enjoyed many a meal of shellfish. So we may conclude that canoes passed across the East River at this point, and that goods were transported in this way to Manhattan. Now the natives of Long Island were expert in making the little beads of sewan, which were so much prized by many Indians and which became better known as Wampum. These beads were certainly exchanged for other objects, for they are found in use in faraway places. Exchanges would be made for fur, skins, meat, tobacco, pottery vessels and for tobacco pipes made of baked clay. This exchange seems to have passed through the lower end of Manhattan, a place which was occupied by a relatively small number of Indians of the Canarsee (Kings County) chief-taincy.

To reach the New Jersey mainland the traders must have walked up the Weckquaesgeek Path to Eighth Street, where they went west to the Hudson River near our present Gansevoort Market. There they met traders from other parts of the continent who probably came from across the river to meet them. The place of meeting was known as "Sappohanikan."

Some came from Hoboken or Hobokan—hackingh, "The place of tobacco-pipes," from which name it would seem to have been the place where pottery pipes made of red Jersey clay could be exchanged for beads and probably for dried oysters and other sea food.

Indians were accustomed to travel great distances on these paths, and after the Dutch settled in Nieuw Amsterdam, natives were employed as "runners" to carry letters and messages. They kept up a trot for many hours, covering long distances. On the Albany Post Road there was a place known as

"Apauque-ipis-ink"

meaning, "the place by water where there is a lodge covered with rushes," in which thatched shelter, the runners to and from Albany could take a rest, and drink from the nearby spring of water.

It is now known as Poughkeepsie, and the run each way was no less than seventy-five miles.

It is evident that Indian men must have been careful to keep in fine physical condition, with muscles hardened by constant use and well-developed lungs.

XIV
VILLAGE LIFE

*"Around the site of each native settlement, little paths branched out to all the nearby sources of food and supplies. The most used, and therefore perhaps the widest, was the way to the spring or to the bank of a brook, on which trail at some time daily the whole community and even the village dogs traveled to quench their thirst.

Through the underbrush some path always led to a nearby planting ground, trod by patient women workers of the soil, or by a cheerful crowd combining to gather the ripened corn or to bring in the daily supply of beans and squashes. In the summer season other of the women folk could be seen making their way on narrow trails through the woods to gather the wild fruits in brake and thicket, the strawberry, the wild cherry, and the blueberry, or in the fall to collect mushrooms and other fungi, to shake down the hickory nuts and walnuts, or in early spring to tap the maple for its sweet sap.

Down at the marsh, while the men were snaring mink or shooting bullfrogs or blackbirds, the girls were gathering roots of sweet-flag, or scratching up the arrow-leaf tubers and artichokes, to fill the vegetal larder.

The elder boys were out on slender bypaths in the wild woods gathering sumac and bark for their elders to smoke, and helping

---

* This description is taken from "Indian Paths in the Great Metropolis," published by the Museum of the American Indian, Heye Foundation, New York, 1922.

themselves to straight dogwood sticks for their arrowshafts, or with the willing aid of the family cur, chasing the rabbits or scratching out the woodchuck from his lair.

You could find most of the old men around the bark houses doing a little light labor, repairing arrows and bows, carving bowls and spoons of wood, and fitting handles to tools; and possibly some were fixing gourds with rattles of wild-cherry pits or Jack-in-the-pulpit seeds, or were indulging in the adornment of their persons with paint-stone or dyes of blood-root and sumac.

The old women would be out on another pathway that led to the flower banks where grew the herbs for medicine, scent, and dyes, the mallows and burdocks, ground cedar and pennyroyal, the wild mint and sage, and roots of sweet-flag and cicely.

Perhaps the shaman might have been found on some lonesome footway looking for materials for ceremonials or charms or potions; love roots and lucky seeds, cedar and sweet-grass for incense.

The arrival of the canoes at nightfall after a day's fishing or oystering was the signal for the villagers to crowd the path to the landing-place, whence in "notassen" of woven grass and basswood fiber, they aided the men to land the catch of oysters and fish; or when the whoop of the returning hunters echoed through the darkening forest, to run on the main trail to meet them, as on boughs of ash they carried the welcome venison to the smoking village fires, freshly kindled in anticipation of their success."

De Vries, who was a firm friend of the natives, wrote of them in his Journal; "They gather their maize and French beans the last of September and October, and when they have shelled the corn they bury it in holes which they have previously covered with mats, and so keep as much as they want in the winter while hunting."

These food pits have been found on every village site, usually filled with the discarded shells of oysters.

In some cases they were utilized as graves. In one such pit at Snakapins village on Clauson Point, there was a human skeleton flat on its back with two heavy boulders on its chest. It looked

STEATITE JAR FROM QUEENS COUNTY, NEW YORK.

66a

POTTERY JAR, 5¼ INCHES HIGH, FROM PELHAM BAY PARK, NEW YORK CITY.
BOTH PHOTOGRAPHS COURTESY OF THE MUSEUM OF THE AMERICAN INDIAN, HEYE FOUNDATION

A SHELL PIT

THIS IS ONE OF THE PITS ON THE VILLAGE SITE EXTENDING ALONG THE HILL AT SEAMAN AVENUE, MANHATTAN. IT WAS EXPOSED BY OPENING IT ON ONE SIDE, LEAVING ITS CONTENTS OF OYSTER SHELLS IN PLACE. IT WAS EVIDENTLY AN EXCAVATED PIT, WHICH WAS AT FIRST USED TO STORE FOOD. AFTER THE FOOD WAS WITHDRAWN IT WAS UTILIZED AS A RECEPTACLE FOR DISCARDED SHELLS OF OYSTERS, WHICH DURING PART OF THE YEAR FORMED THE MAIN ARTICLE OF FOOD FOR THE NATIVES. THE LARGE STONE PROBABLY SECURED A COVER OF THE PIT AND FELL IN WHEN THE WOOD OR BARK DECAYED.

as if the unfortunate being had been cast backwards into the pit, and crushed with the stones.

A number of pits have been explored on the extensive site recently discovered at Throg's Neck, on either side of East Tremont Avenue. They were filled with discarded shells, chiefly those of oysters. In most of these pits there have been more or less broken pottery, and in some there were traces of a fire. The pottery is varied in character, form, and in decoration, so we gather that each pit contained the debris of a lodge or dwelling, into which was cast the fragments of a vessel when it was fractured; and it follows that such a household disaster was a not infrequent occurrence.

The pits are usually found disposed on sloping ground, and as they are not regularly arranged we may assume that they were used and filled from time to time, and when thus occupied, another was dug nearby. Close to a group of such pits we found a skeleton, which appeared to be that of a female, buried in an unusual fashion, that is, laid out in a straight posture on its back. We have assumed that this was an interment of relatively late date, since it evidences acquaintance with the European method of burial of a corpse, which would lead to the conclusion that the village was occupied after white settlers had arrived.

In village sites at Mariners' Harbor, on Staten Island, there were pits in which there were remains of cobs of corn, of beans, and of nuts and these had been charred by fire. These had been filled with food materials which the natives expected to utilize, but were destroyed or burned by Dutch troops who raided Staten Island in an expedition designed to punish the natives for the murder of white settlers.

XV
FIRE

THE natives of this region had learned the use of fire. It was produced in one of two ways; either by a spark derived from the striking of one hard stone on another, or by patient frictional rubbing of two pieces of wood together. The latter method was accomplished by twirling a stick between the hands, and pressing its point until it cut into a slab of soft wood and finally produced the temperature of fire. Such a slab was carried by hunters or bowmen, by which means they could light a fire and cook food, when absent from the fire-pit of their home.

Once the flame was secured and a fire kindled, it became a feature of domestic life to keep the lodge-fire alight. The fuel being wood, a supply of cut firewood must always have been on hand, and the housewife was ever on the alert to see that the fire was alive.

On several village sites, notably at Clauson's Point and at Throg's Neck, in the Borough of the Bronx, we have found near the center of the settlement, the ashes of a very extensive fire pit, which we assume may have been a village community fire, to which any woman could go and get a light, or on which she could heat a cooking vessel when the domestic fire had burned out. This was probably quite a civic improvement in its way, and it was evidently a great convenience, for we have found that the women had brought earthen pots and had heated their food on these communal fires. Some of the pots had broken, perhaps getting overheated, and hundreds of fragments of the broken vessels lay among the ashes.

68a

DRYING MEAT

THE PRESERVATION OF MEAT WAS OF GREAT DOMESTIC IMPORTANCE, CARRYING A FAMILY THROUGH THE SEASON WHEN NO MEAT WAS OBTAINABLE.

THE MEAT WAS DRIED BY HANGING IT, IN THE CARCASE OR IN STRIPS, FROM A FRAMEWORK OF POLES, HIGH ENOUGH TO KEEP DOGS, WOLVES AND WILD CATS FROM REACHING THE MEAT, AND IN OUR CLIMATE A SMOKY WOODFIRE UNDERNEATH WOULD DRIVE AWAY THOSE ANIMALS AND KEEP AWAY INSECTS. IN HOT CLIMATES THE SAME PRACTICE IS FOLLOWED, BUT THE MEAT IS DRIED BY THE HEAT OF THE SUN.

68b

Over the level land of Queens and Kings Counties, the grasses grew waist high, through which elk and deer grazed at will. Every spring the natives fired the stubble.* This was a dangerous practice, though much practiced by the Canarsee and the Rockaway, for it must have often got out of control, and the fire then destroyed the standing timber. The idea was to clear the forest and to start grass growing, in order to attract deer, but whether it did so or not, it opened up the floor of the forest so that the white immigrants could find their way from place to place. Fire was also used to fell trees, the woodsman smearing clay to restrain the smouldering fire. By the same agent they burned out the interior of a log when forming it into a canoe. They used fire to heat stones, for we have found many stones which show signs of having been heated. These hot stones were employed for various heating purposes, to cook food, or to boil water or heat soup. Hot stones also heated little cabins in which they sat or crouched, and perspired before plunging into cold water nearby. These little shacks or cabins were made with a frame of boughs of trees, covered or plastered with clay. Sometimes a solitary native, sometimes men, women and children lay down inside, and when heated to perspiring, crawled out and jumped into cold water. This process cleansed their bodies, and was considered also to be a remedy for rheumatism.

----

* Denton, Daniel and Ogilvy, John.

XVI

OF DOGS

MANY of the Indians of New York City were the owners of a pet dog, which they called "Mekane." Some of the remains of these dogs have been found, carefully buried, evidence of the regard in which the animal was held.

The dogs were sturdy beasts, wolf-like in appearance, and were bred from wolves that had been captured when young, and tamed. Charles Wolley described them as "Young Wolves Stolen From Their Dammes."

In the Indian household they were doubtless highly esteemed. They acted as a watch, kept off prowling wild beasts, and aided the hunters in rounding up deer. There were no domestic cats, so we may imagine that the bark huts had many visitors in the form of rats, field mice and chipmunks, which the dog may have helped to keep under control.

Among many varieties of food, the natives occasionally ate a dog, but in several burials of dogs, a skeleton has been found to be intact, so the animal's body must have been placed in its grave complete. In the graves of dogs at Seaman Avenue, on Manhattan Island, there were skeletons of different proportions, and once the author came upon the skeletons of two small dogs, probably pet puppies, which had been laid at the bottom of a pit on the sand and were carefully covered over with oyster shells. Indians were afraid of savage dogs. When the raiding party assassinated Anne

Hutchinson and her family, they first persuaded one of her servants to tie up the dogs which protected the household.

Skeletons of dogs have been found buried at Inwood on the Island of Manhattan, also at Van Cortlandt Park on the site of the Indian village of Mosholu, and on a village site of Siwanoy natives in Pelham Bay Park, in the Borough of the Bronx.

Pope, the English poet, wrote of the Indian's conception of the future life . . . who

> "thinks, admitted to that equal sky
> His faithful dog shall bear him company."

XVII

OF IMPLEMENTS

SOME stone tools used by the Indians of New York are of materials which do not exist within the area of the metropolis, and it may be assumed that our natives obtained those objects by trade and barter. It has thus been said with some justice that there is a greater variety of material and workmanship in a handful of our local native objects than in a much greater quantity in other localities. We can see this variety by examining native artifacts found within the area of the Greater City, wherein there will be seen points made of jasper from New Jersey, and of chert of which no supply exists within the bounds of the City. Some objects came from great distances. On Fort George Hill the petrified tooth of a shark was found, which was naturally formed like an arrowhead, and this probably came from as far as South Carolina.*

The materials from which these points were made are of wide variety. Chert or flint afforded the best results, and must have been in wide demand.

In a number of places, and in one Indian site near Fort Hamilton in Brooklyn, a deposit has been found, of partially completed leaves of chert or flint, which were probably buried for the purpose of "ripening" the material. The quarries from which the stone was extracted were carefully and quite extensively worked by natives. They were not situated in or near New York City.

As observed in a Vermont quarry, the material was broken into

---

* The Indians of Manhattan Island, Skinner, p. 251.

STONE KNIVES

THE KNIFE WAS A MOST IMPORTANT IMPLEMENT IN INDIAN EXISTENCE, USED FOR MANY PURPOSES, IN WHICH WE CAN READILY INCLUDE THE KILLING AND SKINNING OF GAME, CUTTING UP MEAT AND SKINS, CARVING PLATTERS AND CUPS OUT OF WOOD, SCALPING ENEMIES, PREPARING FOOD, AND CUTTING CORN-COBS.

THEY WERE USUALLY MOUNTED ON SOME KIND OF HANDLE, THOUGH WE HAVE FOUND SPECIMENS THAT COULD HAVE BEEN HELD IN THE HAND, WITH A RAZOR-LIKE CUTTING EDGE PROJECTING.

THESE ARE SPECIMENS FOUND WITHIN THE AREA OF THE METROPOLIS.

72a

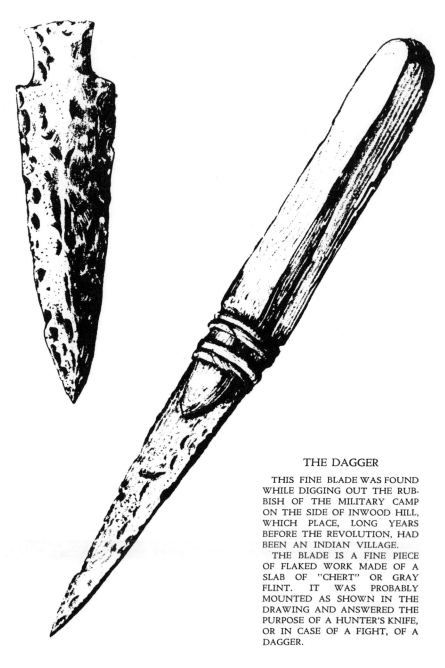

THE DAGGER

THIS FINE BLADE WAS FOUND WHILE DIGGING OUT THE RUBBISH OF THE MILITARY CAMP ON THE SIDE OF INWOOD HILL, WHICH PLACE, LONG YEARS BEFORE THE REVOLUTION, HAD BEEN AN INDIAN VILLAGE.

THE BLADE IS A FINE PIECE OF FLAKED WORK MADE OF A SLAB OF "CHERT" OR GRAY FLINT. IT WAS PROBABLY MOUNTED AS SHOWN IN THE DRAWING AND ANSWERED THE PURPOSE OF A HUNTER'S KNIFE, OR IN CASE OF A FIGHT, OF A DAGGER.

72b

blocks by heavy stone mauls or hammers, and these were then split, chipped or cracked into flat slabs of leaf shape about the size of the hand. In this form it appears that the blanks or leaves were traded away to natives, who carried them away and worked them into the forms they desired.

In this way material probably traveled considerable distances, and many of the tools and weapons found on Indian sites in the area of the City of New York constructed of materials from distant places, were worked into shape where they were used.

We may be justified in assuming that the natives of the City made good use of the attractive beads of sewan, by securing in exchange for them, the products of many other localities. The materials which were bartered included pottery, which would account for our discovery of vessels of evident Iroquoian make, and having a variety of incised decorations, most of which are of the same tribal origin.

The necessities of existence must have demanded constant attention. De Laet, who wrote on the subject in 1625, had observed some of the native habits, and he described their use of earthen pots for cooking, the large leaves which they used as saucers, the mussel shells which served as spoons, and ladles formed of dried calabash. We have some reason to suppose that the shell or carapace of the tortoise, which has been found near discarded rubbish, was also used as a spoon or ladle. They wove mats of reeds or of the husks of corn, binding them together with the stringy stalks of maize. They also wove a string or thread of "Indian hemp" from the dogbane plant, of which they made ropes, which in later times they sold or traded to the European settlers. Of this thread they made "Bags, Purses, or Sacks which they call 'Notas', which word signifies a Belly, or anything hollow." "Their cordage is so even, soft and smooth that it looks more like silk than hemp."

In fact, any natural object which answered a practical purpose was, we may be sure, utilized by these people. Fortunate it was for them, that Nature in New York was so bountiful a provider.

Indian objects often are seen, scattered over the surface of their once-occupied house sites. It is probable that the tools and implements were thrown aside when the white man's superior appliances came into the natives' possession.

We have been sometimes surprised to find quantities of broken pottery, fragments of vessels which were very necessary to their existence, and the construction of which involved considerable work and skill. Broken vessels were repaired by making small holes on either side of the fracture, through which thongs could be passed and the broken edges drawn together. Probably with the addition of a little clay smeared into the fracture, the vessel would hold together and answer some useful purpose.

But we can readily imagine how useless those vessels became, when the Indian housewife had become the possessor of a metal cooking-vessel.

Similarly the best stone knife became a worthless implement alongside of the steel blade, and arrows and bows were discarded as soon as a gun and powder could be procured. It is therefore probable that objects picked up on the surface date from the period of the natives' contact with white colonists.

Those objects buried under shells or soil cannot be accounted for in the same manner. They were lost or discarded in the course of existence a long time before Hudson appeared upon the scene. They invite careful observation of their position relative to other objects, and of their form of construction which may have become antiquated in bygone years. A greater historic and ethnological interest therefore attaches to buried objects than to those picked up on the surface of an Indian site.

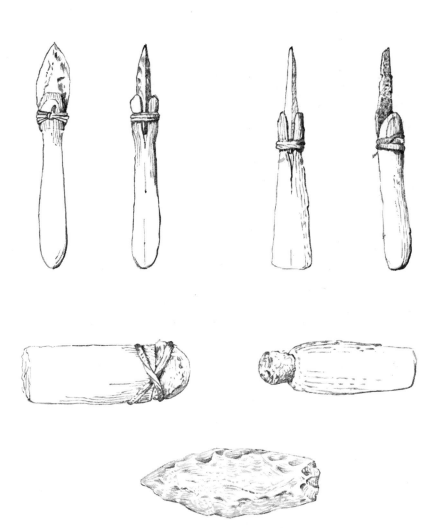

SCRAPING TOOLS

MANY STONE PIECES WHICH ARE COMMONLY CLASSED AS "ARROW-POINTS," WERE DESIGNED FOR THE NECESSARY DOMESTIC USE OF SCRAPERS. THE PIECES HERE SHOWN WERE ALL FOUND WITHIN THE AREA OF THE CITY OF NEW YORK, AND WERE PROBABLY HAFTED AS SHOWN IN THE DRAWING.

THEY WERE USED IN VARIOUS SCRAPING OPERATIONS, TAKING THE FLESH FROM THE SKINS OF ANIMALS, AND FROM BONES, ALSO FOR SHARPENING STICKS AND BONE IMPLEMENTS.

SOME PIECES WERE MADE OF A FORM SUITED TO BE HELD IN THE HAND, WITH ONE SHARP SCRAPING EDGE. SOMETIMES A BROKEN ARROW-POINT WOULD BE FLAKED OFF FOR USE AS A SCRAPING TOOL.

74a

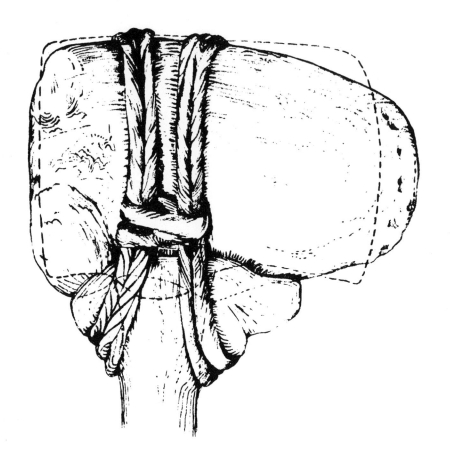

THE AXE

THE STONE AXES OF THE INDIANS WERE OF VARIOUS SHAPES BUT WERE ALWAYS MADE WITH INCREDIBLE PATIENCE AND DETERMINATION. THE STONE PEBBLE OR SLAB WAS PECKED WITH OTHER SHARP POINTED STONES UNTIL IT ASSUMED THE APPROXIMATE SHAPE OF AN AXE HEAD. THEN IT WAS RUBBED AND GROUND UNTIL IT TOOK ON THE FINISHED SHAPE. THE SPECIMEN ILLUSTRATED WAS FOUND ON MANHATTAN ISLAND. IT IS FORMED WITH TWO GROOVES WHICH LENT THEMSELVES TO FASTENING THE HEAD TO THE HAFT, BY TWO THONGS. THE CUTTING EDGE WAS NEVER VERY KEEN, AND THE INDIAN WOODSMAN OR CARPENTER DEPENDED MAINLY ON THE USE OF FIRE TO EAT AWAY THE WOOD, WHICH THE AXE SUPPLEMENTED.

THE AXES BROUGHT OVER FROM EUROPE WERE TOO LONG AND TOO LIGHT FOR THE HEAVY LUMBER AND HARD WOODS OF THE AMERICAN TIMBERLANDS. THEY WERE OFTEN BROKEN AND THEIR BLADES WERE THEN USED AS WEDGES. THE EUROPEAN AXES WERE TRADED WITH INDIANS WHO FANCIED THEIR SHARP CUTTING EDGE; BUT THE EUROPEAN SOON LEARNED FROM THE INDIAN AXE, THAT THE SHORT BLADE AND THE HEAVY "POLL" WERE NECESSARY. THE AMERICAN FORM OF AXE WAS THUS DEVELOPED, AND TO ITS USE IN CLEARING THE FOREST WAS LARGELY DUE THE SETTLEMENT OF THE AMERICAS.

74b

XVIII
THE AXE

THE European settlers brought with them the tools with which they had been accustomed to work in their home countries. The axe was an indispensable implement, probably in those days the most important. But European axes were suited to the relatively small timber of old countries, or adapted to cutting and felling soft wood trees such as the pine and the fir.

When those axes were put to work to fell the enormous trees then growing in the wild forests of America, they proved to be ill-adapted to the hard woods and to the deep cuts required in clearing the woodlands for cultivation and settlement. European axes were long in the bit and had little weight in the poll. We have found their broken blades, which had been afterwards utilized as wedges in splitting up felled timber.

The natives of the vicinity of New York City had made for themselves axes of stone which, however poor they may have been or unsuited to cutting the wood, were nevertheless formed in a practical manner, with a heavy weight at the head or poll, which drove the sharp flaked edge into the timber.

The drawing, Plate XIII, shows such a stone axe, which was found at Inwood on the island of Manhattan, to which has been added the thongs which must have bound it to the haft or handle in Indian style. On this drawing an axe blade of early American form is shown in dotted lines, exhibiting its similarity in shape. The white settlers may have thus learned from the Indian the way to adapt the form of their axes to the needs of felling the heavy timber, which was required to effect the clearing and settlement of the American continent.

The stone axes of our natives were products of considerable skill and of unlimited patience. They were first pecked into rough shape from a pebble or stone of suitable size, and by a long and tedious process were then rubbed or ground on other stones to a smooth finished surface. The groove was similarly pecked and ground, and the head thus finished was so formed as to be secured to one or other form of handle or haft. There were several methods of such mounting of the axe-head, evidenced by the shape of the head or the grooving around it.

It has been said that the successful clearing of the forests was the achievement which was most effective in bringing about the settlement of America. The conqueror of the forested wilderness was the American Axe, and its efficient design was attributable in no small part to the craftsmanship of the Indian.

CELT FROM FLATLANDS, LONG ISLAND, NEW YORK.
GROOVED AXE FROM LINCOLN PARK, NEW JERSEY. *PHOTO-*
GRAPH COURTESY OF MUSEUM OF THE AMERICAN INDIAN,
HEYE FOUNDATION

76a

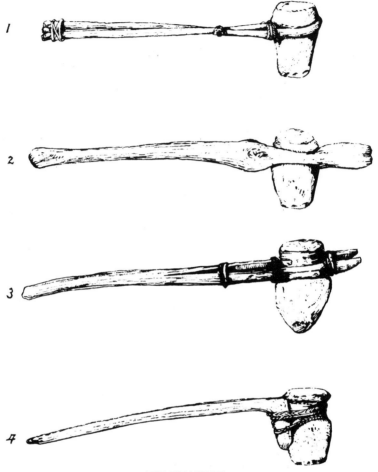

AXE HANDLES

THE METHODS ARE HERE SHOWN, BY WHICH STONE AXES OF INDIAN WOODSMEN WERE PROVIDED WITH A HANDLE.

1—PERHAPS THE MOST COMMON FORM, IN WHICH THE AXE-HEAD IS GROOVED ALL ROUND THE STONE.

2—IS AN AXE HEAD FITTED INTO A HOLE FORMED IN THE SHAFT; THE WOOD BEING SOAKED IN WATER WOULD TIGHTEN AROUND THE STONE, MAKING A VERY SECURE FASTENING.

3—HERE THE HEAD IS GROOVED ONLY ON THE TWO SIDES AND IS SECURED IN THE CLEFT OF A SPLIT STICK BOUND SECURELY WITH SINEWS OR THONGS.

4—APPLIES TO THOSE AXE-HEADS WHICH HAVE A FLAT BACK, TO WHICH A BENT STICK, OR "KNEE" COULD BE FITTED AND LASHED TO THE STONE BY THONGS.

76b

XIX
ARROWS

ALL pointed stones are not arrow-points, for many were made for other uses. Every form of cutting tool was necessarily made of flaked stone. Many so-called arrows are really short knives designed to be fastened to a stick or they are scraping tools used to scour flesh from the skins of animals which were afterwards utilized as clothing.

Some blades were very keen, some were basil-edged, others were serrated or toothed, making keen cutting knives, some of which were carried by hunters and were used to kill or skin animals, and others were probably utilized in conflict or for the purpose of scalping.

Many of these implements were cast away after the white settlers' lighter and more serviceable steel knives came into Indian possession. We may judge of the attractiveness of such steel weapons or tools by the number which were used in bartering the land of the City and its vicinity.

Of all the possessions of the white man, the steel knife seems to have been that which was most in demand. A list of all the objects for which the area of the County of Westchester was conveyed to white settlers, shows that knives were the most numerous. More than three hundred knives headed the list, followed by one hundred and eighty-five axes and hatchets. Next came one hundred and forty-one hoes and a hundred and seventeen kettles or cooking pots.

In the use of the bow and arrow Indians were very skilful, and one observer noted that even a boy of seven years of age was dexterous enough to shoot a bird on the wing. "Little boys with Bowes made of little sticks, and arrowes made of great Bents will hit down a piece of tobacco pipe every time a good way off."

In order to avoid the loss of a stone arrow-point, the point was formed and fastened to its shaft in such a manner that the shaft with the arrow-head firmly attached by a lashing of thongs and the use of resin could be withdrawn from the wound it had created. Such points are "stemmed," formed with a stem or projection by which they were fastened. The type of arrow-point which was intended for use in war (developed, it is believed, by the Iroquois nation) was in the form of a wide triangle, fastened rather insecurely to the shaft by a thong. If the shaft were pulled out of a wound, the head might be left in place, whereby the wound would be more likely to prove fatal. Arrow-heads used in war were sometimes treated by dipping the stone in the poison of rattlesnakes. Indians are credited with such a cruel purpose and were supposed to be the originators of the practice of driving a nail into a leaden bullet, with the purpose of creating a fatal wound in the victim. Such a practice, however, was in use even as late as the War of Independence, when bullets with nails driven in them, were found in possession of Connecticut soldiers, so that the natives are not to be regarded as wholly responsible for the practice. The idea seems to have been a precursor of the invention of the "dum-dum" bullet and other murderous methods of human cruelty.

The arrow, like other flaked objects, was made by first chipping a block of suitable stone into a rough blank, and then flaking off pieces at either side by the use of a bone or horn tool. The blank was held in one hand, and the tool applied with the other hand. The bone tool being caught under a projecting edge, a strong sudden jerk would cause it to flake off.

A support was sometimes used for the tool, which was set in a handle so as to rest upon the support. In this way a very powerful

ARROW POINTS, CELT AND PIPE FRAGMENTS. CLAUSON POINT, BRONX, NEW YORK. PHOTO-
GRAPH BY ALANSON B. SKINNER, 1918. COURTESY OF THE MUSEUM OF THE AMERICAN INDIAN,
HEYE FOUNDATION

BONE AWLS, BEAD AND FISH HOOK. CLAUSON POINT, BRONX, NEW YORK.
PHOTOGRAPH BY ALANSON B. SKINNER AND COURTESY OF THE MUSEUM OF
THE AMERICAN INDIAN, HEYE FOUNDATION

78b

jerk could be applied to the flake, which was probably necessary in the formation of large objects.

Some of our natives must have become very expert in this kind of craftsmanship, and were regularly employed upon it. There are evidences of the manufacture of tools, in abundant chips and flakes of stone scattered around some places.

The patient effort and accumulated skill which these stone artifacts required is only faintly to be realized by us who enjoy the advantages of mechanized conveniences and modern labor-saving devices.

XX
HUNTING AND FISHING

THE men who went fishing or hunting took with them a supply of food, usually a baked corn-cake. The hunter must start on his quest as early in the morning as possible. We may imagine that the chase would often take him very far away from his home, and his food supply might give out, but hungry though he might be, he must continue until he could secure some animal for his family's sustenance and clothing. Then, carrying the heavy load on his shoulders, he must make his way back through the forest to the trail that led to his home.

To keep himself in condition to undertake such arduous work, was then the first consideration of the male Indian, and his weapons were next in order. He not only had to keep these sharpened, but had to provide himself with new arrow-points and new shafts to take the place of those lost or broken during the chase. His skill was also used in making "traps or gins," in which beaver and other small animals were caught. Furthermore in the hunter's passage through the wild forest he was constantly exposed to danger. Rattlesnakes swarmed in the rocky places, vipers and moccasin snakes in the swamps. The hunter had to know the snake-root or other herbs that were used as a remedy for a snakebite. If he had a companion, the latter would suck the poison out of the wound. The hunter had learned from childhood the ways and habits of the wild creatures of the forest. He could imitate their call or cry, and entice the animal within range of his bow by many devices.

Wild animals probably became scarce in the area of New York City, and hunters must have traveled long distances into the forests of Westchester County, of New Jersey, and of the Ramapo mountain region to find their quarry. So it was natural that the natives should have recourse to fish food, which was in plenty at their door. Shell-fish seem to have been very abundant around the shores of New York waters, and in early times they grew to prodigious size. Therefore, the sites of one-time Indian settlements are found to be strewn with the discarded shells of oysters, the deposit sometimes being piled a foot or more in thickness. Only here and there among the shells and among the ashes of wood fires do we come across a piece of bone, showing an occasional meal of meat. Some of the ancient oyster shells found near the shore, especially in the Bronx, are eight inches in length, each oyster a meal in itself. We have observed that among myriads of oyster shells, there were few of the clam, and rather rarely scallop or mussel shells.

Indians were accustomed to break meat bones in slivers in order to get the marrow out of the interior. Many of these fragments of bone are found, some showing marks of teeth, which may have been those of rodents. Perhaps the family dog was treated occasionally to such a dainty. But compared with oysters the fragments of bone are relatively scarce.

Large fish such as sturgeon, were speared. Some of their scales have been found in food-pits. With small arrow-points mounted on slender shafts, the fishermen also shot fish under water. We find that our natives knew how to make nets, for there are impressions in the clay of which earthenware pots were made, that show the pattern of a net. It is also related by an eyewitness that they had nets of very large proportions. We also find many grooved stones that served as net-sinkers. The floats were made of dried sticks, cut into suitable lengths. So it is certain that fish were caught in quantities by the use of nets. The bones of some kinds of fish are sometimes found among the shells. These were probably used as needles. Large bones of the cat-fish were sometimes strung together

81

and used as a breast ornament. A complete set of fish bones composing such an ornament of fishbones was found in a food-pit at Inwood.

We find impressions of a coarse basket-ware woven of rushes. These receptacles were called "Napsas," and were used to carry oysters and fish from the boats to the villages or to convey the products of the soil from the planting-ground.

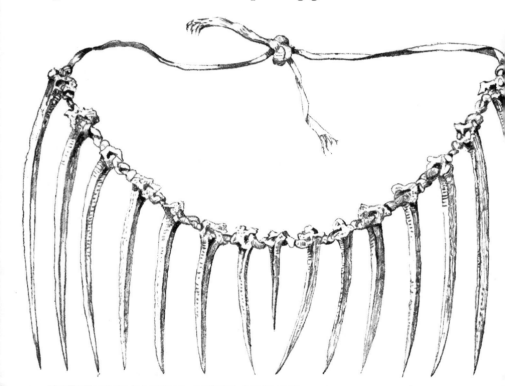

BREAST ORNAMENT

THESE CAT-FISH BONES WERE FOUND CLOSE TOGETHER IN A SHELL-PIT AT INWOOD, MANHATTAN, AND WHEN CLEANED AND ASSEMBLED IN THE FORM OF THE DRAWING, THEY APPEAR TO HAVE BEEN STRUNG TOGETHER TO FORM AN ORNAMENT, FOR WHICH THE OPENINGS IN THE HEAD OF EACH BONE MADE THEM READILY AVAILABLE.

THE PRACTICE OF USING SUCH AN ORNAMENT IS REFERRED TO IN THE WRITINGS OF B. B. THATCHER, WHO, IN HIS "INDIAN BIOGRAPHY," PUBLISHED IN 1832, QUOTES FROM AN EARLIER AUTHOR THE FOLLOWING LINE OF POETRY:

"THE CURIOUS FISH-BONES O'ER HIS BOSOM SWUNG."

XXI
HOMES

THE patience and perseverance of Indians were great. Felling a large tree was a long and tedious job. It was accomplished only by burning away the wood, and then chopping and scraping away the charred materials.

The fire was confined by the use of clay or mud so that it burned or smouldered only within the space enclosed by the clay. In this way the woodsman burned into a tree trunk and then with smashing force, drove the edge of his heavy axe into the charred wood.

The bark was preserved in large slabs, and was utilized in forming a covering for their homes. Our Indians had developed quite an ingenious method of constructing a house far superior to the "wigwam" of western tribes where bark for such a covering could not be procured.

They bent saplings over and lashed their tops together to form an arch. Then they planted flexible poles in a line and bent them over, so that they thus constructed the frame of an arched building. They lashed poles across these arches, using the strips of fibre under the bark of the elm, and perhaps some ropes made of the dogbane, or of twisted cat-tail rushes. Over this they fastened sheets of bark tied together like shingles, pegged with sticks and plastered with mud, the upper layer held in place by stones, or slabs of rock.

In this way they made quite a serviceable shelter, and they became so skilful that these houses were made long enough to accommodate a number of families. They are said to have been sometimes more than a hundred feet in length, quite a "tenement house." With all their skill and ingenuity, they failed to construct a chimney, in which matter they were as backward as the Romans of old.

One of these Indian habitations was visited by the travelers Dankers and Sluyters in the fall of 1676. It was situated at the Indian station known as Nayack, near Fort Hamilton, Brooklyn.

They found in this dwelling seven or eight families, comprising about twenty persons. Their description follows:

"Their house was low and long, about sixty feet long and four-teen or fifteen feet wide. The bottom was earth, the sides and roof were made of reed and bark of chestnut trees, stuck in the ground and all fastened together. The ridge of the roof was open, about a half a foot wide from end to end, in order to let the smoke escape, in place of a chimney. On the sides of the house, the roof was so low that you could hardly stand inside it."

"The entrances which were at both ends were so small that they had to stoop down, and squeeze themselves to get through them. The doors were made of reed or flat bark."

Of the domestic life within the house these writers observed:

"They build their fire in the middle of the floor, according to the number of families, so that from one end to the other each boils its own pot, and eats what it likes, not only the families by them-selves, but each Indian alone when he is hungry at all hours, morning, noon and night. By each fire are the cooking utensils, consisting of a pot, a bowl or calabash, and a spoon also made of calabash."

The smoke from the fires inside these bark houses found its way out only by a hole in the roof, and the inside of the house was sometimes chokingly full of smoke. The smoke had one practical advantage, for insects were driven out, and the all-present mosquito was discouraged from disturbing the occupants.

Moreover, the residents were none too clean, and the smoke may have helped to keep down vermin of all kinds. It is, however,

A CIRCULAR BARK-COVERED HOUSE

THIS FORM OF HUT IS SOMETIMES DESCRIBED AS A "BEEHIVE," WHICH IT RESEMBLES IN FORM. IT WAS INGENIOUSLY FORMED BY A FRAMEWORK OF CURVED TREES AND PLANTED POLES BENT OVER AND LASHED TOGETHER. THE BRACING BY DIAGONAL POLES EXHIBITS CONSIDERABLE INGENUITY. THE FRAME WAS COVERED WITH STRIPS OF BARK OR GRASS. MATS AND SKINS COVERED THE ENTRANCE. MUD WAS USED TO CLOSE CRACKS AND CHINKS. THE CENTER WAS LEFT OPEN TO EMIT SMOKE FROM THE FIRE, WHICH WAS KINDLED IN A DEPRESSION IN THE FLOOR, AND SURROUNDED WITH A FENCE OF STONES TO GUARD AGAINST FLYING SPARKS.

STONES WERE PLACED ON THE SHEETS OF BARK TO KEEP THEM FROM FLAPPING OPEN IN THE WIND.

THIS ROUND HUT WAS DEVELOPED INTO THE "LONG HOUSE" FORM, THE SHAPE OF WHICH WAS DERIVED FROM THE IROQUOIS.

84a

THE LONG HOUSE

THE INGENIOUS METHOD OF SHAPING A BEEHIVE DWELLING WAS EXTENDED TO A LARGER FORM OF SHELTER, DOUBTLESS TO AFFORD A RESIDENCE TO AN INCREASED POPULATION.

THE SAME METHOD WAS USED, OF ERECTING A FRAMEWORK OF BENT POLES, INCLUDING SOMETIMES A HANDY GROWING SAPLING, AND BY EXTENDING THE FRAME IN A HORIZONTAL DIRECTION A LONG ARCHED FRAME WAS PROVIDED, TO BE COVERED AS WAS CUSTOMARY WITH LARGE SHEETS OF BARK HELD IN PLACE BY THONGS OR STRIPS OF SKIN, BY ROPES OF REEDS, OR TWISTED CORN-STALKS. THE UPPER SLABS OF THE COVERING WERE SECURED BY STONES, SO THAT THEY COULD BE MOVED TO AFFORD AN OPENING FOR THE SMOKE OF THE FIRES. IN SUCH "LONG-HOUSES" SEVERAL FAMILIES MADE A HOME, AND KEPT THEMSELVES WARM BY PLUGGING THE CREVICES WITH CLAY, AND PILING BUSHES AND CORN STALKS TO KEEP OUT THE WIND.

84b

probable that the smoke had some effect on the eyes, and may have injured the eyesight to some extent.

Around the house-fire the family gathered to eat their meals, to rest, and to sleep. They sat squatted on grass mats or lay sleeping on heaps of reeds* with feet stretched out towards the fire, covered only by their clothing and some skins of animals. But, as Roger Williams wrote:

> "God gives them sleep on Ground on Straw,
> On Sedgie Mats or Board."

Their fare was poor, their life had many hardships, and sometimes they knew hunger and privation, but the bark-hut was Home.

AN INDIAN VILLAGE OF THE MANHATTANS.
prior to the occupation by the Dutch

PHOTOGRAPH FROM VALENTINE'S MANUAL. 1858.
COURTESY OF THE MUSEUM OF THE CITY OF NEW YORK

---

* Richard Blount, 1687.

85

XXII
THE CAVE DWELLING

We still possess, and fortunately in public ownership, one of the most ancient, as well as the most picturesque of the homes of the aborigines. On the extreme northerly end of the island of Manhattan, in a deep glen in Inwood Hill Park, there is to be seen a cave formed by fallen rocks, in which Indians for a long time made a home. The interior was nearly filled with soil, washed in by the rains of two hundred years of disuse, when the curiosity and enterprise of Alexander Chenoweth was aroused by the small remaining space, into which he began to delve.

Becoming interested in the evidences of aboriginal life in that locality, he came across the upper part of the opening of the cave hidden in the woods. This he proceeded to enlarge, and soon came upon broken pottery in considerable quantity. Digging downwards, he found the ashes of fires, one below the other, with much broken pottery and some stone tools. These indicated the use of the cave as a dwelling at intervals of time, during which the cave was invaded by soil washed in by the rains and melting snows.

The fragments of pottery when reunited formed some large vessels of Algonkian type, indicating the use of the cave as a dwelling, long before the arrival of the white man. These vessels are now to be seen in the American Museum of Natural History. The Cave has been carefully cleared out to the level of the original floor by the Dyckman Institute, appointed Curator by the Department of Parks.

THE CAVE-DWELLING

THE SLABS WHICH WERE PEELED OFF THE BLUFFS OF INWOOD HILL BY FROST AND BY
MELTING WATERS OF THE GLACIAL AGE FELL INTO "THE CLOVE" OF INWOOD HILL PARK.
AND SOME FALLING ACROSS EACH OTHER, FORMED A CAVERN WHICH WAS UTILIZED FOR
A HOME BY NATIVES OF MANHATTAN.

THIS CAVE WAS NEARLY FILLED WITH SAND AND SOIL WASHED INTO ITS INTERIOR BY
LONG SEASONS OF RAIN AND MELTING SNOWS, WHEN ALEXANDER CHENOWETH DUG INTO
ITS INTERIOR AND FOUND INDIAN TOOLS, FIREPLACES, AND BROKEN POTTERY VESSELS WHICH
HAVE FOUND A PERMANENT HOME IN THE AMERICAN MUSEUM OF NATURAL HISTORY. THE
POTTERY WAS OF EARLY FORM, ALGONKIN TYPE, INDICATING THE USE OF THE CAVERN IN
THE REMOTE PAST.

THE ENTRANCE OF SUCH A DWELLING WAS UNDOUBTEDLY COVERED BY SKINS SUSPENDED
ON A POLE. WITH CLAY OR MUD TO STOP UP THE CREVICES, AND A GOOD WOOD-FIRE ON
THE HEARTH, LIFE INSIDE THE CAVERN WAS PERHAPS MORE COMFORTABLE THAN EXISTENCE
IN A COLD WATER FLAT.

86a

INDIAN ROCK DWELLING NEAR COLD SPRING, MANHATTAN. IN A CLOVE
NEAR SPUYTEN DUYVIL CREEK, THIS ROCK DWELLING WAS FOUND TO CON-
TAIN ABORIGINAL POTTERY, TOOLS, BONES, ETC., PROVING LONGTIME OCCUPA-
TION BY TRIBES ANTECEDENT TO THEIR SCATTERING BY THE MOHAWK
INDIANS IN 1673. *PHOTOGRAPH COURTESY OF THE MUSEUM OF THE CITY OF
NEW YORK*

86b

There are also exhibited a splendid vessel discovered at 214th Street, by W. L. Calver, and many other objects, discovered around the Inwood district on the Island of Manhattan, of native origin. Others may be seen in the Museum of the American Indian, Heye Foundation, at 155th Street on Broadway, where they can be compared with a great collection of similar objects used by various native tribes in all parts of the Americas. The Museum of the City of New York exhibits some interesting and instructive specimens.

Near the Cave there are overhanging rocks, which formed a shelter for some of the natives, for we found the ashes of fires there, with shells and fragments of bone.

There is also nearby, a small space under one overhanging rock in which the upper layers of discarded refuse contained objects of European origin, such as clay pipes, fragments of china-ware, and lead bullets. These things make it clear that some of the Indians continued to reside there long after the arrival of the white invaders, and that they secured some materials from them. This confirms the record of history, which informs us that natives in that vicinity remained there until 1715, when they were induced to remove by payment to them of a sum of money.

XXIII

OF CANOES

THE natives around the City of New York did not use birch-bark canoes. They carved their boats out of a log of timber by burning and scraping the inside, and by hacking and scraping the outside into the shape of a boat. This process made a stout, heavy canoe, well suited to the wide spaces of water over which they had to travel, for sometimes they came around the coast from the south shore of Long Island, passing through the rollers of the ocean along the shore of Coney Island, and carrying quite heavy loads in the boat, or a number of passengers.

We have not found their paddles or their oars, but it is supposed that they were made of wood, of about the same type as other Indians used. They stood upright in the canoe while paddling.

Roger Williams, of Providence, observed the methods which the natives of that region employed in fashioning a boat. "I have seane," he wrote, "a Native goe into the woods with his hatchet, carrying onely a Basket of Corne with him, and stones to strike fire—when he had felled his tree (being a Chestnut) he made him a little House or shed of the bark of it—he puts fire and followes the burning of it with fire in the midst . . . so he continues burning and hewing until he hath within ten or twelve dayes (lying there at his work alone) finished."

There is a careful drawing which was made about 1630, showing some Indians in their boats near New Amsterdam. The boat in the foreground of this picture, which is being propelled by four

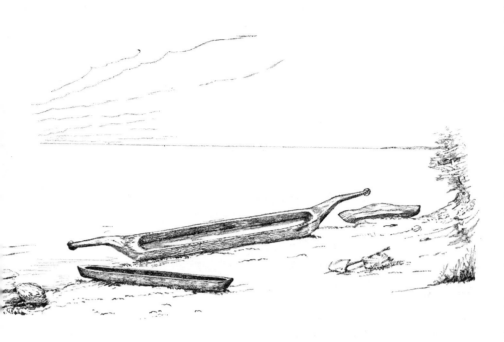

BEACHED

(MAHELO OR AMOCHOL)

THESE BOATS ARE ALL FORMED OUT OF TREE-TRUNKS HOLLOWED BY FIRE, AND WERE HACKED INTO SHAPE BY THE STONE TOOLS OF THE INDIANS.

THE LARGE BOAT WITH THE PROJECTING POINTED EXTENSIONS HELD A NUMBER OF MEN, AND THE PROJECTIONS WERE DESIGNED FOR LIFTING THE BOAT. THERE IS RECORD OF SOME OF THE LARGER CANOES MAKING THE JOURNEY TO ROCKAWAY THROUGH THE ATLANTIC ROLLERS, AND IT MAY BE THEREFORE THAT SUCH LARGE CANOES WERE USED FOR DEEP-SEA TRAVEL AND PERHAPS FOR HUNTING WHALES OFF THE COAST.

THE LITTLE CANOE WITH THE HUMP IN ITS SIDE WAS A STOUT CONVEYANCE FOR A SINGLE FISHERMAN, AND THE LONG DUG-OUT IS OF THAT TYPE OF WHICH SEVERAL HAVE BEEN FOUND PRESERVED IN THE MUD OF THE MARSHES AROUND NEW YORK.

THE PADDLES WERE SPADE-LIKE IMPLEMENTS PATIENTLY CARVED OF WOOD.

88a

ort nieuw Amsterdam op de Manhatans

THE FIRST KNOWN PICTURE OF NEW AMSTERDAM, MADE AROUND 1626 BY CYRN FREDERICKSZ FOR THE DUTCH WEST INDIA COMPANY. THE PICTURE IS REVERSED BECAUSE THE ORIGINAL ENGRAVING WAS PROBABLY MADE WITH THE AID OF A *CAMERA OBSCURA,* WHICH PRODUCED AN INVERTED IMAGE. THE CORRECT VIEW WITH GOVERNORS ISLAND AT THE LEFT AND THE MILL ON THE WEST SHORE OF MANATTAN IS OBTAINED BY LOOKING AT THE PICTURE IN A MIRROR. *PHOTOGRAPH COURTESY OF THE J. CLARENCE DAVIES COLLECTION, THE MUSEUM OF THE CITY OF NEW YORK*

88b

Indians, with a coxswain shouting orders, has peculiar elongated projections at the bow and the stern.

Another canoe of less size, with the same kind of projections, is in the middle distance, propelled by two native women.

This form of vessel is also drawn upon the map of "Novi Belgii," under which is written: "Navis ac arboris tranco igne excavata," or "Vessel made from the trunk of a tree hollowed out by fire," which is precisely the method which was employed. The projections seem to have been made for the purpose of lifting and carrying the boat.*

The canoes of which some have been discovered whole or in part in and near New York, are of much simpler form. They consist of a straight flat-bottomed craft, rounded or pointed at both ends, a mere hollowed log. This was the kind of canoe most in use on the quiet waters around the City.

There seem to be two Lenape words for a canoe—Mahelo and Amochol, which may have been applied to different forms such as we have described, much as we might differentiate between a boat and a barge. A ship was described as "Rena Maholo." A large type of canoe, propelled by six men, was used in hunting whales off the Long Island coast. This dangerous process required two boats, and each would have "an Harpineer and a Steersman."

Dankers and Sluyter observed in 1676 that the Canarsee natives' fishing canoes were constructed "without mast or sail, and not a nail in any part of it, though it is sometimes fully forty feet in length."

They used "scoops to paddle with, instead of oars."

---

* "Aboriginal use of Wood in New York," Beauchamp, New York State Museum Bulletin, 89.

XXIV
WILD LIFE

Wild animals lurked in the woodlands which covered the larger part of the interior of the present boroughs. They were doubtless more prevalent in the Bronx than elsewhere, because that part of the City is on the mainland, and packs of wolves could make their way south from the dense forests of Westchester County, driving the deer before them. Around the region of Eastchester, the earliest settlers paid a bonus for the slaughter of wolves, and made a number of wolf-pits in which those obnoxious creatures were trapped.

There were wolves and bear on Manhattan island as late as 1686, when the settlers in New Harlem organized a general hunt through the forests of Washington Heights and killed them all.

Deer were scarce in Brooklyn, perhaps because they had to find their way through the lands of the Rockaway in Queens, and to run the gauntlet of wolves and wild cats, as well as Indian hunters.

Beavers made a home along the small rivers such as the Bronx or Aquehung. In their capture the native hunter took "great pains and pleasure" and made use of traps and gins of his own invention to secure the wary little animals. They continued to make their ingenious homes along the course of that little stream for nearly two hundred years after Hudson's arrival.

Hunting was sometimes practiced in company with others.

De Vries relates that on occasions a hundred natives or more would assemble, and spreading through the woods about a hundred

90

paces apart, would drive the game ahead by beating a stick upon a flat bone.

There is a picture in Champlain's account of the natives of Northern New York, printed in 1609, showing this method of driving the game in precise detail. Each of the natives engaged in driving the wild creatures through the woods, is beating upon a shoulder-blade bone, with another bone such as a shin-bone.

In this way they would herd the wild creatures towards the edge of a river or lake on which others in canoes were in waiting. They would then kill off a considerable number of wild animals, as thoughtlessly as their kinsfolk in the west slaughtered the bison, eventually depriving themselves of a valuable source of food supply.

This drawing also shows the method of trapping animals by bending over a tree by a rope, secured to a stake driven into the ground, and released by the animal incautiously stepping upon a plate which released the rope. A noose at the end of the rope, laid flat on the ground then caught the creature by its leg and the tree thus suddenly released, lifted and suspended the victim, held fast by the noose.

Bear were hunted through the woods of New Jersey and were highly valued for meat and clothing. Some Indians have shown a particular regard for Bears, which were supposed to have some spiritual character.

Skinner observes that all the Algonkians, with whom he had come in contact had "special observances connected with the chase of the bear.* These included the preservation of the skull by placing it on a pole or in a tree, and the bones of the animal were usually protected from the village dogs. The teeth were sometimes worn as an amulet or ornament.

Wild cats must have been an unmitigated nuisance, howling round the villages at night, and destroying small game and birds. Our Indians hunted and ate every kind of bird. As one Dutch

---

* Publications of the Museum of the American Indian, Heye Foundation, Vol. V, No. 4.

writer said, they ate eagles "and similar trash." . . . Everything that could be considered edible was of value to a people who may often have been short of food, sometimes starving. So the muskrat, the bull-frog, the snake and the tortoise all went into the cooking pot, sometimes without any preparation.

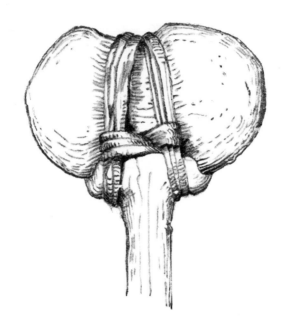

A CLUB

THE STONE CLUB WAS A TERRIBLE WEAPON, IF MOUNTED ON A HANDLE AS SHOWN. AT CLOSE QUARTERS A VIGOROUS MAN COULD HEW HIS WAY THROUGH OPPONENTS WITH SUCH AN IMPLEMENT.

THIS CLUB, MADE OF A STONE CAREFULLY GROOVED ROUND ITS MIDDLE, WAS ONE OF THE NATIVE OBJECTS FOUND IN INWOOD HILL PARK, MANHATTAN.

IT APPEARS TO HAVE BEEN FITTED TO A HAFT OR HANDLE OF WOOD IN THE MANNER SHOWN IN THE DRAWING.

XXV
CLOTHING

BEFORE the arrival of white men, and the exchange of food or furs for European clothing, the natives wore little covering on their bodies, except in very cold weather, when they wrapped themselves in the skins of deer, bear, and other animals with the fur turned outwards in winter.

They went barefoot, and the upper part of their bodies was naked, and but for the grease and fat with which they anointed their skins, they would have been much sun-burned or blistered. Women wore a scanty skirt, otherwise their bodies were bare, as well as their legs. They wore their hair, left to grow as it would, sometimes braided and treated with bear grease.

As for the children, we may suppose that they ran about quite naked in warm weather, and in the cold, they huddled round the fire, wrapped in a furry bearskin or warm deerskin.

If Verrazano's description applied to the Lenape, we may learn that the natives did not differ much from those he had seen in southern waters, "being dressed out with the feathers of birds of various colors." When Juet saw them, more than eighty years later, he also discovered that some used feathers as "mantles." The mantle was used chiefly by women.

Birds in this region were numerous. The turkey, the fish-hawk, the heron, the wild goose, and the pileated woodpecker, blue jay, kingfisher, passenger pigeon, the quail, crows, ravens, hawks and eagles swarmed in the woodlands, while ducks, geese, herons and rails haunted the waters and marshes.

Juet, who wrote the log-book on Hudson's ship, observed that in September "they go in deerskins, loose well-dressed, some in mantles of feathers, and some in skins of divers sorts of good furres."

The Indian men wore a long piece of dressed skin, passed between their legs and tied around the waist by a snake's skin or a cord, the ends hanging down in front and rear. In cold weather women wrapped a bear or coonskin around them, which was sewed with hemp thread and was skewered together with sticks. In the process of stitching these skins, women became proficient. Their needle was a sharpened bone, a fishbone or a thorn, with which a small hole was pierced in the material. The thread was twisted and moistened to a point which was then pushed through the hole. Skins were thus drawn together into a size sufficient for a garment, the opening of which was secured by passing a small stick like a skewer through holes punched in the edge.

Their feet were protected by a strip of hide, or sometimes by corn husks or even by rushes bound to the feet and ankles.

At its best, the protection of skin clothing seems inadequate when we consider the vagaries of our climate, "the heat of parching summers" alternating with "the searching cold of piercing winter, and the tempestuous dashings of driving rains."

They utilized grease as a protection, anointing their bodies with "the Oyl of Fishes, the fat of Eagles, and the grease of Rackoons," as a preventive of blistering by the scorching sun, an "armour against the Muskettos," and an additional protection against the bitter cold of winter.

XXVI
PERSONAL ADORNMENT

Some description of the natives of our region was printed after the arrival of the white settlers, which probably describes their ways with some accuracy, for they were not much given to change in habits.

Women ornamented their skirts with wampum beads, and they wrapped their otherwise naked bodies with a deer-skin, the edges of which were fringed. Their hair they worked into a plait, over which they drew a ringlet of deer's hairs colored red, "whereof they were very vain." They had bracelets and necklaces of beads. They used to wear moccasins and leggings of hide "before the Hollanders settled here," and some made shoes of straw, or foot protection of corn husks.

It is thought that some of the stone or slate slabs, perforated with little holes, were bound in women's hair as an ornament. As a general rule both men and women were bareheaded.

Young girls covered only the lower part of the body and often went naked in any kind of weather. In summer, men and boys wore nothing but the hide which we have described, tied around the waist, the flaps hanging down in front and behind.

In winter, the skins of bear, wolf, beavers, and wild cats were wrapped around their shoulders, and some females made a cape of birds' feathers.

The men took all kinds of trouble and went through some very painful processes to get rid of hair on their faces and on their heads.

They probably shaved with some of their very keen flint knives, sharp flakes of flint, or the edges of shells, but sometimes they would singe the hair off their heads with hot stones. The roach or bristle left on the crown of the head we have already noticed. De Vries says it was like a cock's comb. Hair of the beard was often plucked out from the roots hair by hair.

Their desire for a shaven appearance is as hard to account for as some of the habits of mankind today.

The men were accustomed to paint their faces, and part of their bodies, with colors, of which the easiest to obtain was a red. It was widely used to color the back part of the head. The red color was an oxide of iron, or iron rust, probably obtained from nodules of that metal picked up on the seashore, or perhaps secured by trade with other tribes. Ochre, an earth colored with the same oxides, provided a yellowish pigment, and black was easily obtained from the soot of the household fire. The colors thus used to besmear their faces had considerable significance to the native mind. Wolley wrote that the red color applied to their faces was to them "the sunshine of Peace." We have found several little hollow stones in which there are traces of a red material. Some of these may be "paint-cups" picked up on the seashore, the cavity having been formed by a core which the sea-water had dissolved. This left the stone in the form of a convenient little cup, of which one specimen was found on Manhattan Island at 213th Street.

When thus decorated, with streaks of red oxide, yellow ochre and soot they probably thought themselves highly attractive, but to European eyes, as one Dominie expressed it—they looked "like the devil himself."

Their black hair grew "lank and long," hanging down over their shoulders. It was the fighting men, Warriors and Bowmen who wore the Comb and the Scalplock, and their hair was oiled and frequently dressed.

Some wore pendants, probably made of shells, at their ears,

and others thrust the quill of a porcupine through an orifice drilled through the membrane between the nostrils.

Others painted or scarified their skin with designs, which sometimes represented birds or beasts, doubtless having great significance to themselves and to those who knew of their achievements in warfare or hunting. These decorations were individual adornments that had a meaning for others.

On these personal decorations men spent a good deal of their time, pulling out hair from their faces, shaving or singeing their heads, and trimming the "roach" of hair on their heads. The long lock of hair, which was left dangling from the back of this mane, was the traditional "scalp-lock," supposed to be offered in defiance of their enemies prowess, as much as to say: "Here is my scalp; come and help yourself to it, if you dare."

The women do not appear to have indulged in the practice of fixing their faces, or caring for their complexions—perhaps they were too busy to afford the necessary time. They were, however, fond of necklaces and girdles, as many are in our times. We believe that some of the little beads of "Wampum" were originally made for ornaments, being threaded on a string and used as a necklace.

The natives in general were stately in figure and walked upright, which practice was attributed to their growth as babies when they were strapped or "swaddled" upon a board, and kept in that position for the first year of their existence.

Their hard life, and its elimination of those of weak constitution, was probably more to be credited for their upright carriage, as it was doubtless responsible for their freedom from deformity.

Wassenaer wrote that he knew of few, or none, that were blind, crippled, or deformed.

Their height was between five and six feet, with straight bodies "strongly composed," or as we should say, muscularly developed. Their color was hard to describe, the Reverend Charles Wolley considered them to be true "Adamites," a scholarly reference to

97

the old tradition that Adam was given by his creator a reddish color to distinguish him from other created animals.

Of this finely developed race, Roger Williams wrote in 1643:

"Boast not proud English, of thy birth and blood
Thy Brother Indian is by birth as good."

GORGET FROM LONG ISLAND, NEW YORK, WHICH WAS USED AS PERSONAL ADORNMENT BY THE INDIANS. *PHOTOGRAPH COURTESY OF THE MUSEUM OF THE AMERICAN INDIAN, HEYE FOUNDATION*

XXVII
SEWAN OR WAMPUM

Long Island, to the natives was known as "Meht-anaw-ack," or "Ear-shell-country," a name indicative of the prevalence of conch-shells along its shores. This name is mis-spelled in a number of variants—of which Matona or Mattenwake appear in historical works.

The Island was later described as "Sewan-hacky," or "the land of Sewan," but this name appears to be of Dutch origin. The beads of shell, perforated and highly polished, were held in regard by many Indian peoples.

The abundance of clams and conch-shells along the shores of Long Island provided ample material for the manufacture of these beads, and some of the natives became very expert in shaping and boring the beads, which, as we have seen elsewhere, were traded for other needed materials. The beads became known as Wampum, which is a word of Indian origin, meaning "white string," indicating the use of beads strung on a thong or cord. But the use of the beads among the natives, prior to the arrival of white men, was not as European money is used, that is, as a currency carrying a fixed value.*

It was doubtless traded away by the Rockaway and the Canarsee, but its real value seems to have been on a higher level, for it was regarded as the substance of a highly appreciated gift, which when given by one Indian to another was a significant demonstration of

---

* "History of the County of Westchester." Bolton, Robert, Vol. 1.

good faith and friendship. Thus when a bargain was made, we find that a string of the beads was given by the buyer to the seller, not as a part of the price, but as an evidence of good faith and good intentions accompanying the transfer of property.

When a conference took place between the natives of a differing nationality, the selected speaker after announcing his people's views, would hand to his opponent a string, or on very important occasions a belt, made of the beads. Then the opponent would make an oration, and would hand to the other speaker a string or belt of at least equal character.

Both parties were thus assured of the clear and binding nature of any agreement which was the result of the conference, and they preserved the beads as an evidence of the agreement. It will be apparent that the beads thus served, in the absence of writing, a very important purpose.

The beads varied in color, in size, and in the accuracy of their finish. The work is supposed to have been done largely by women, and, in the absence of any steel tools, we can imagine that the cutting, polishing, and above all, the boring of the little beads required unlimited patience and experienced skill.

Each bead thus represented a certain quantity of human energy and patient craftsmanship and very soon after the white settlers arrived, they began to assume a commercial value. White buyers of food and land soon perceived that the Indians regarded the beads as of greater importance even than their European tools and kettles, and since they had to acquire the beads by purchase or barter, the settlers soon came to place a monetary value upon them. The white beads being more readily made from the shell of the conch, were more common, and therefore, of less established worth than purple beads, which could be made only from the thick blue portions of shells, which in our district were chiefly those of the hard-shell clam or "quahog."

Thus sewan or loose beads began to pass from hand to hand, and the name of Wampum came to be applied to the strings of

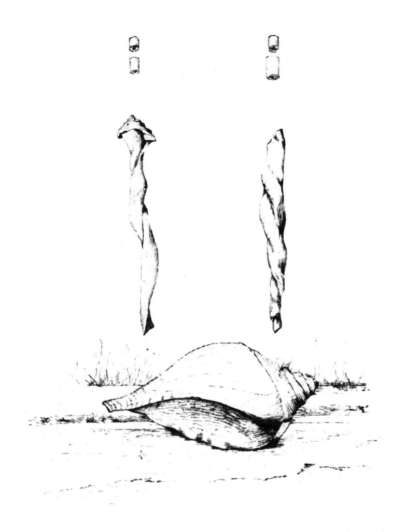

WHITE WAMPUM

THE CONCH SHELL DERIVES ITS NAME FROM THE LATIN "CONCHA" WHICH SIMPLY CONVEYS THE IDEA OF A SHELL. THESE CONCHES HAVE A SPIRAL CORE OR COLUMN INSIDE, WHICH WHEN BROKEN OUT FORMED THE MATERIAL FOR THE WHITE BEADS KNOWN AS WAMPUM OR SEWAN.

THE SHELLS WERE COMMON OBJECTS ALONG THE SEASHORES AND ARE SAID TO HAVE BEEN PARTICULARLY IN EVIDENCE AT OYSTER BAY, ON LONG ISLAND. ON SEVERAL INDIAN SITES WITHIN THE CITY OF NEW YORK, WE HAVE FOUND A NUMBER OF THE SPIRALS KNOCKED OUT OF THE CONCH SHELLS, LAYING CLOSE TOGETHER, AS IF THE WORK OF PREPARING SHELL-BEADS WAS IN PROGRESS.

100a

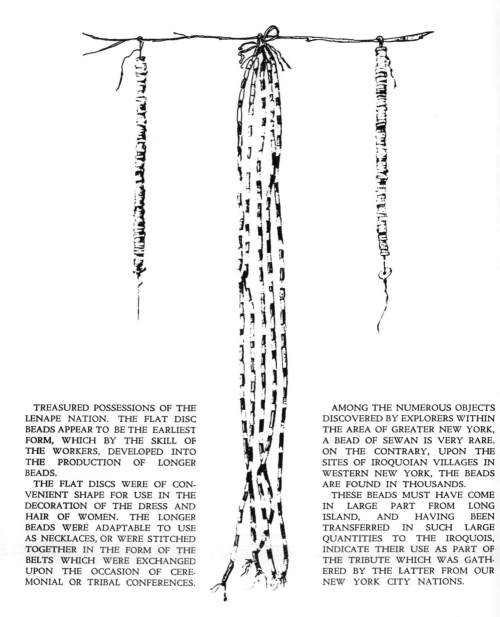

TREASURED POSSESSIONS OF THE LENAPE NATION. THE FLAT DISC BEADS APPEAR TO BE THE EARLIEST FORM, WHICH BY THE SKILL OF THE WORKERS, DEVELOPED INTO THE PRODUCTION OF LONGER BEADS.

THE FLAT DISCS WERE OF CONVENIENT SHAPE FOR USE IN THE DECORATION OF THE DRESS AND HAIR OF WOMEN. THE LONGER BEADS WERE ADAPTABLE TO USE AS NECKLACES, OR WERE STITCHED TOGETHER IN THE FORM OF THE BELTS WHICH WERE EXCHANGED UPON THE OCCASION OF CEREMONIAL OR TRIBAL CONFERENCES.

AMONG THE NUMEROUS OBJECTS DISCOVERED BY EXPLORERS WITHIN THE AREA OF GREATER NEW YORK, A BEAD OF SEWAN IS VERY RARE. ON THE CONTRARY, UPON THE SITES OF IROQUOIAN VILLAGES IN WESTERN NEW YORK, THE BEADS ARE FOUND IN THOUSANDS.

THESE BEADS MUST HAVE COME IN LARGE PART FROM LONG ISLAND, AND HAVING BEEN TRANSFERRED IN SUCH LARGE QUANTITIES TO THE IROQUOIS, INDICATE THEIR USE AS PART OF THE TRIBUTE WHICH WAS GATHERED BY THE LATTER FROM OUR NEW YORK CITY NATIONS.

SEWAN OR WAMPUM BEADS

100b

beads which were exchanged. Finally the Dutch authorities fixed an actual monetary value on the beads by establishing the relation between Dutch "stivers" or pence and a certain number of the beads. As soon as that was done, the beads became the equivalent of money, and Indians, armed with little steel awls or "muxes," as they were called, turned out quantities of beads, while some white people also made a large quantity of beads of poor and uneven quality, some with holes only half perforated.

Many years later a factory was established at Pascack, near Paterson in New Jersey, where an ingenious mechanic made a little drilling machine capable of boring seven beads at once. This machine with its steel drills is still in existence. It could bore much longer holes with accuracy, and by its means some long beads or "pipes" were made which were extremely attractive to Indians. These long beads were formed out of the column of shell in the center of large conch shells. The beads found their way from one tribe to another to the far West, and may sometimes be seen today in the possession of Western Indians.

All these developments came from the patient work of our Indians of New York City and its vicinity, and it is interesting to reflect that the center of the business of trading, in those primeval days, was the same island of Manhattan which was to become in our time the financial centre of the great metropolis of modern trade into which the City of New York has developed. The beads are very rare in the Indian sites in the vicinity of the City, but have been found by thousands in the Iroquois region.

Van der Donck wrote in 1656, concerning the making and the use of shell beads:

"The species are black and white, but the black is worth more by one-half than the white. The black wampum is made from conch shells (he was wrong, for that kind of wampum was made from the purple center or lip of the clam) which are to be taken from the sea, or which are cast ashore from the sea, twice a year.

101

"They strike off the thin parts of those shells, and preserve the pillars or standards, which they grind smooth and even, and reduce the same according to their thickness, and drill a hole through every piece and string the same on strings and afterwards sell their strings of wampum in that manner."

De Vries observed that the natives would fasten beads to their ears, and the women would wear a string of beads around their necks or twine it in their hair.

Sometimes they would ornament a garment with beads, much as the more modern Indian uses glass beads for the same purpose. Others made bands of the beads to be worn around the arms. We can observe that the love of the beads has been a characteristic of women of all ages, and it may well have been that the Indian woman's desire for such a personal ornament may have originated the difficult process of making beads.

Strings were fastened together, in which form they were used around the body, and were known as "belts." Single strings of beads were used in trade and in the conveyance of land, and were measured by the "fathom."* The "belts," often ingeniously arranged so as to form a design or pattern of purple beads among white beads, were passed from hand to hand on very important occasions, such as conferences between tribes. Some of the most interesting "belts," which were given on historic occasions, are to be seen in the Museum of the American Indian, Heye Foundation.

---

* A measure which involved three hundred and sixty white beads, or an equivalent of one hundred and eighty black or purple beads.

XXVIII
FIELD AND FARM

Our Indians, in fact all the Indian tribes, were industrious and successful farmers. We are indebted to them for their labor in cultivating and improving those staple articles of food—the potato and "Indian-corn" or maize, and hardly less for the gift of tobacco. We may reflect that these products of nature were grown, were improved by the selection of seeds and of plants, and were cultivated in the most suitable manner by the simple and uneducated Red Man.

Much of the work of farming was done by women, so it is probably to women that the world owes the possession of the potato and of maize as food, and of the tobacco plant as a solace, or a habit, according to the use we make of it.

Maize or Indian corn is supposed to have been developed by slow stages and by the exercise of infinite care and patience, from a plant, "Zea Mays" of weed-like growth, which is native to tropical America.* By selection and cultivation the Indians of North America developed several varieties of the corn, differing in the shape of the kernels, in their color, and in taste. The corn cob in those early days was not so long as it became in later times, and was more pointed.

Each permanent settlement appears to have had, not far from the lodges, a "planting field," the ground being carefully selected and skilfully cultivated. At a suitable time when the corn had a

---

* Cyclopedia of American Horticulture. L. H. Bailey, 1902.

103

good start, beans were planted which used the cornstalks as poles. Between the corn the squashes and pumpkins sprawled, so that no part of the cultivated land, so hardly won, lacked some useful purpose.

The soil was prepared by using a stone hoe, of which many specimens have been found, varying in size and shape. They usually consist of a wide pebble split or pecked into shape, or of a piece of rock flattened on one side. The blade was usually wide enough to make a good furrow or to rake up a hill in which the seeds were planted, and it was mounted on a hooked stick, to which it seems to have been lashed by thongs of skin or gut.

There are instances of the use as a hoe of the shoulder-blade of some animal, but the form most used in the area of New York City, is a flat slab of stone, chipped or flaked to provide a rough groove for a thong to bind it upon a handle. The handle appears to have been made of a sharply bent stick, such as could be cut from a sapling growing more than one stem.

Our natives were quite skilled in growing beans, of which they had developed several varieties of different colors. These beans were used to flavor the corn-meal, which must have become a rather commonplace article of food. They grew squashes and pumpkins, and they raised or gathered the wild grape, which they dried into currants. Tobacco was one of their products, which Hudson's crew found to be "strong and good for use."

There were very few of the products of nature of which the Indians failed to make use. Every edible berry, root or nut became part of the food supply, every herb that had some medicinal quality was searched out in its hiding place in the wild woods. When the white settlers arrived they must have been to a very great extent dependent upon the natives for food, and they certainly must have had many things to learn about the trees, plants, flowers, and fungi that grew in the new country, rich as it was in many of nature's products that were strange to European eyes.

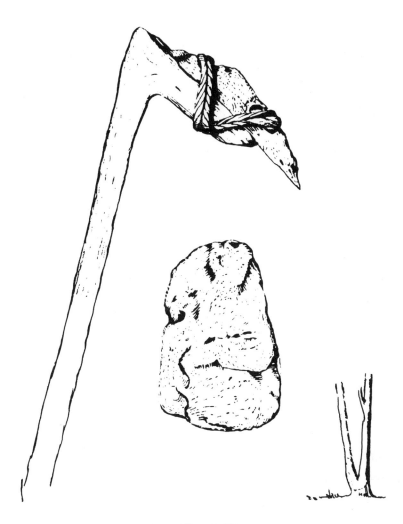

THE INDIAN HOE
FOUND AT INWOOD

THESE TOOLS WERE MADE IN VERY ROUGH FORM, AND HAVE BEEN FOUND
IN MANY PLACES WHERE LAND WAS CULTIVATED. ANY FLAT STONE COULD BE,
AND WAS, USED FOR THE PURPOSE. THE METHOD OF SECURING THE HOE-BLADE
TO A LONG STAFF, IS SHOWN. THE FORKED SUPPORT WAS CUT OUT OF A TWIN
TREE OR BUSH, AS ILLUSTRATED ABOVE. WHEN TIED IN PLACE, WITH A DEER-
SKIN THONG, AND WITH A WOODEN WEDGE DRIVEN BEHIND THE BLADE, IT
MADE A RATHER SERVICEABLE IMPLEMENT, THOUGH VERY HEAVY TO HANDLE.
THE NATIVES WELCOMED THE LIGHT EUROPEAN HOE, WHICH APPEARS AMONG
THE ARTICLES FOR WHICH THEY TRADED AWAY THEIR HOMELANDS.

104a

TOBACCO

THE USE OF TOBACCO FOR SMOKING WAS AN
INDIAN HABIT, AND WAS FOUND BY THE FIRST
EUROPEAN VISITORS TO BE PRACTICED AMONG THE
VARIOUS PEOPLES WHO INHABITED THE EAST COAST
OF OUR COUNTRY. THE TOBACCO PLANT IS A DE-
VELOPMENT OF INDIAN AGRICULTURE. IT CAN BE
GROWN IN THE REGION OCCUPIED BY THE CITY OF
NEW YORK AND WAS DOUBTLESS GROWN BY OUR
NATIVES, WHO BROUGHT BUNDLES OF THE LEAVES
TO HUDSON'S SHIP.

THE PIPES USED FOR SMOKING IN AND NEAR
NEW YORK WERE OF TWO KINDS, ONE FASHIONED
OUT OF SOAP-STONE, AND ANOTHER MADE OF
BAKED POTTERY. THE LATTER MAY HAVE BEEN A
MORE RECENT FORM. WE HAVE FOUND PIPES OF
BOTH MATERIALS IN THE WASTE HEAPS OF NEW
YORK CITY.

POTTERY PIPE AND STONE PIPE

104b

And we, to whom some of these things are now so familiar, may be reminded by them of those far-away days when the natives walked along the narrow pathways that are now buried under some of our great buildings and city streets, scenting the sweet odors of flowers and of the wild grape, welcoming the same return of spring that we experience, and listening to the call and the songs of the ancestors of the birds that we can hear warbling in our parks and woodlands.

XXIX
THEIR FOOD

THE food of the natives included anything eatable that came their way. Almost any edible object, grain or flesh, went into the cooking pot. Van der Donck, the Dutch attorney, wrote of this subject in 1649:

"Their fare, or food, is poor and gross, for they drink water, having no other beverage; they eat the flesh of all sorts of game that the country supplies, even badgers, dogs, eagles and similar trash, which Christians in no way regard; these they cook uncleansed and undressed.

Moreover, all sorts of fish; likewise snakes, frogs and such like, which they usually cook with the offals and entrails."
He proceeded to say, however, that:

"They know also, how to preserve fish and meete for the winter, in order then to cook them with Indian meal."
The missionary, John Heckewelder, who lived among the Lenape of Pennsylvania at a later date, tells in much greater detail of their method of preparing food. He says that "The Iroquois are said to have been formerly very dirty in their eating," but that the Lenape were cleanly and "even delicate."

He tells a story of how the natives, with whom he was staying, produced a dead wild-cat which they pretended to cook and to serve as a meal. This was really an Indian practical joke, and they would have enjoyed immensely the spectacle of the missionary making a meal upon such fare, but he was too wise, he refused the proffered meal and later deer meat was provided and the cat's carcass was thrown away.

In the waters of the New York City area the natives found an abundant supply of food.

Hudson said that they caught all kinds of fish with seines, young salmon and sturgeon. We have found scales of sturgeon in food pits, so that we may suppose that in those days the rivers swarmed with fish.

In the shallows the oysters grew in incredible numbers and, particularly along the shores of the East River, to immense proportions. Clams and scallops added to the variety of fish food.

Their vegetable food included the maize, the beans and the squashes cultivated in the planting fields, and many nuts, berries and roots which they gathered in the woods. The corn, especially, was a staple article of their larder. They boiled meat with it, or made a bread, the "corn-pone" of our southern States, and a porridge which was called "Sapsis," sometimes flavored with beans, and sweetened at times with maple sap or maple sugar.

They cooked squashes in a pot covered over with large leaves to prevent the steam escaping. The corn they pounded into a coarse flour, then it was kneaded into a dough, and having, of course, no yeast with which to raise the dough, it was baked into a "flap-jack," about an inch thick. The bread was rendered more palatable by mixing with the meal beans or chestnuts, sometimes dried meat.

Corn was cooked in other ways, after being ground to a coarse flour by a stone "pestle" in a hollow stone or "mortar," or pounded with a heavy wooden pestle in a mortar made of a hollowed-out section of a tree. Our natives knew how to grind it fine into a real flour, but they usually produced a rather coarse meal. This was mixed with water into a dough, and baked among hot ashes into a "pone," a flat cake very convenient to carry and gnaw. Sometimes, perhaps very often, corn kernels were eaten in a raw state. We have found Indian skulls in which the teeth have been

107

ground off by constant chewing of some hard material. This was probably corn that had not been cleaned of sand.

The corn meal was also thinned out into a kind of porridge, which they called "Sapsis," a word containing the syllable "Samp" —a name which is still applied to boiled corn in our Northeastern States. The thinnest mixture made a soup, in which the housewife placed pieces of meat, or of any edible thing that happened to present itself, such as a bird, a turtle, a frog and even a snake. Real hunger knows no nicety; sometimes any kind of edible object was acceptable. William Wood in his "New England's Prospect" wrote in 1639:

> "The dainty Indian maize
> Was eat with clam shells out of wooden trays."

and he adds, metrically, that the Indian cook sought the luscious lobster, mussel, periwigge, oyster and tortoise, dived for cockles, and dug for clams.

Indians have always been skilful in carving wood and Hudson observed the use of wooden bowls, colored red, in the meal at which he was entertained in the Iroquois region.

Meat was dried to provide food at times when it would be scarce. In hot climates the rays of the sun were sufficient for this purpose, but in our climate the meat was most probably smoked by lighting a fire under a rack or frame on which the meat was hung. The smoke answered the double purpose of desiccating the flesh, and at the same time discouraged the flies, and probably kept wolves and dogs at a distance.

On the whole, we may assume that the household meals were somewhat varied, though there were doubtless occasions when there was very little to eat, and even the children went hungry. Indian children were, however, trained to fast, and to get used to going without food for days at a time.

Daniel Denton tells how plentiful were the fish in all the streams and in the waters of the locality. He tells also of seals, which in "innumerable multitude" during the winter crowded upon the beaches and the sand bars of the coast of Long Island. We see such sights no more.

De Vries tells of their method of fishing, with seine nets "from seventy to eighty fathoms in length which they braid themselves."[*]

Their sinkers were stones, of which many examples have been found, sometimes neatly grooved to receive a cord for attachment to the net.

He observed that, over the mouth of the net the natives would fasten a figure of wood, which he thought resembled the devil. When the figure began to move by the fish entering the mouth of the net, "then the fishermen would call upon the 'Mannetoe', that is, the devil, to give them many fish."

"They also catch in little set nets, six or seven fathoms long, braided like a herring net. They set them on sticks in the river, one and one-half fathoms deep."

[*] De Vries Journal, p. 162.

XXX
OF STRING AND THREAD

THE natives of the region of the City of New York had developed some domestic manufactures.

The housing and clothing of themselves and of their children required some form of cord or thread. The inner part of the bark of "slippery elm" afforded a coarse, flexible, fibrous material which was used in binding together the parts of their dwelling houses, and for purposes requiring a considerable degree of strength, a thong could be readily formed of a fine strip of skin. For binding or securing stone blades on their shafts, there was no better material than skin or gut. But for making nets, a natural vegetable fibre was desirable, and the "hempe" of which Juet's record tells us, was made from the fibre of the dog-bane plant, which has sometimes been called "Black Indian Hemp." Out of the milkweed plant another form of fibre could be obtained, and when twisted together such vegetable fibres made a string or cord that would be serviceable in the form of a net. The women brought such "hempe" to Hudson's crew.

The stitching process in binding skins for use as clothing must have been very slow and laborious. Many little "perforators" have been found, some made of bone and some of stone, the use of which was to make a hole in the skins through which a string could be threaded. Each hole had to be made before a thread could be drawn through. William C. Orchard, an authority upon the details of native needlework, says, "The Indians did not use needles when sewing leather for clothing. With a thread of moistened sinew, an awl of bone, a fish bone or a thorn to make perforations in the leather, creditable sewing was accomplished. One end of the sinew thread was allowed to dry and stiffen. That would follow a perforation even better than a sharp pointed needle."

As to needles, they did not exist, and even after the white man brought a supply, we may believe that they were scarce. We found one at Inwood, Manhattan, made of bone with an eye at the blunt end, which must have been made after the natives had seen a European needle. Bone needles with eyes have been found recently among Indian debris in the Borough of Queens.

Steel needles were among the articles traded by the European settlers in purchasing land, and were doubtless highly prized and utilized by the native women after clothing of European material came into use among them.

Women workers utilized as thread the hair of wild animals, and we read of ornaments on their heads made of the long hair of deer, dyed a red color.

This dye was another of their uses of a product of nature, derived from some vegetable such as sumach, which their woodland skill and keen observation had discovered.

The Indian partiality for bright colors was soon observed by white visitors. Hudson's unscrupulous crew placed red coats on the natives whom they treacherously detained on the Half Moon, expecting apparently that by strutting around in that illuminated garb, they would become reconciled to their abstraction from their native land. However, one of them sneaked off, and the other jumped overboard. Both coats probably disappeared with them.

XXXI
INDIAN ART

THE earthenware vessels, which were made by natives and which were in service in every village, and indeed in every hut or shelter, were objects which were made by women. The same craft exists today in western Indian settlements and is produced by females. Pottery may thus be regarded as a form of original American art, which had been in course of development over a very long period of time. The results of these women artists' skill and patience are evidenced in the beauty and the extraordinary accuracy of shape and perfection of designs which were applied to their surfaces. The variety of styles in the decoration is remarkable. They are evidence of an artistic sense and of craftsmanship of marked character.

Even the earliest type of vessel which we ascribe to the early or Algonkian period, is accurately formed, and in its crude decoration exhibits the desire of the potter to add some kind of interest, or to develop some pleasing effect upon the articles which were to form so important an element in her domestic life. The materials used to make these pots were the clays common in many districts, to which the artist added pounded shells or scraps of mica. The method employed in building up such vessels seems to have been to form a rope of the prepared clay, and to wind this around in a circle, gradually building up the shape of a circular vessel. The clay was then pressed together by the fingers, and was smoothed inside by the use of an oval pebble. The exterior surface was smoothed by hand and was often given a texture by pressing some material on

112

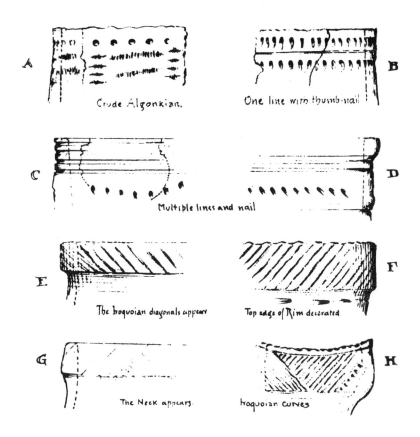

A — Crude Algonkian.

B — One line with thumb-nail

C, D — Multiple lines and nail

E — The Iroquoian diagonals appear

F — Top edge of Rim decorated

G — The Neck appears.

H — Iroquoian curves

DEVELOPMENT OF POTTERY ART OF UNAMI INDIANS

(DRAWN FROM SHERDS RECOVERED ON INDIAN VILLAGE SITES)

POTTERY RECOVERED FROM INDIAN SITES WITHIN THE AREA OF THE GREATER CITY IS OF CONSIDERABLE VARIETY AND EVIDENCES A CHANGE IN DESIGN, BOTH AS TO FORM AND DECORATION, WHICH WAS IN PROGRESS DURING A LONG PERIOD OF TIME.

THE NATIVE PRODUCT BEGAN WITH A SOMEWHAT CRUDE FORM OF VESSEL, HAVING STRAIGHT VERTICAL SIDES, EXTENDING UPWARDS TO A PLAIN RIM, THE EDGE OF WHICH OFTEN LACKED ANY REINFORCEMENT, OR WAS BUT SLIGHTLY FLARED OUTWARDS. IT WAS THUS VERY FRAGILE. DECORATION WAS EITHER LACKING ALTOGETHER, OR CONSISTED OF THE SIMPLEST FORMS OF DEPRESSIONS MADE WITH A STICK, OR SCRATCHED WITH A SHELL. THE GRADUAL CHANGE OF FORM, THICKENING OF THE RIM AND THE INCREASE OF DECORATION IS SHOWN IN THE GROUPS OF SHERDS ILLUSTRATED IN THS DRAWNG.

THE FORM OF DECORATION GRADUALLY DEVELOPED FROM THE HORIZONTAL LINE ENCIRCLING A VESSEL, INTO DIAGONAL LINES AND IN ONE OF THE RAREST FORMS WHICH WAS FOUND AT THROGS NECK, TO VERTICAL GROOVES AND LINES OF FACETS.

THE TOP EDGE WAS PROGRESSIVELY STRENGTHENED BY THICKENING, AND THE SHAPE OF THE VESSELS IMPROVED BY THE FORMATION OF A NECK.

112a

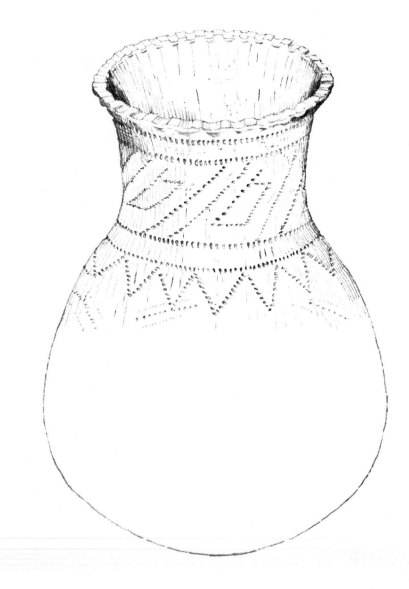

POTTERY VESSEL

SHOWING UNIQUE FORM OF NECK
DRAWN FROM PORTIONS FOUND AT THROGS NECK, 1932

A REPRODUCTION OF THIS VESSEL
BY AIMEE VOORHEES IS IN THE MUSEUM
OF THE AMERICAN INDIAN, 1933

112b

the wet clay, or by dabbing the clay with a stick or bundle of reeds wrapped with a thread or cord. They had no potter's wheel but produced remarkably symmetrical and accurately circular vessels.

The pottery found, in large numbers of fragments or "sherds" scattered around the abandoned fire-hearths of our New York City village sites, is of considerable variety. There are specimens of the crudest material and form of the shapely and carefully decorated productions of the Iroquois, and some specimens of uncommon grace of shape and with elaborate decoration, of which two found recently, at a village site at East Tremont Avenue, Throg's Neck, Borough of the Bronx, are unique.

The oldest or Algonkian form of vessel was a jar, the mouth of which was only slightly expanded, the rim being of the same thickness as the body, and there was little if any treatment of the rim by way of ornament. Nor did the body receive much attention, as it had little more decoration than the impression of a mat, a net, a basket, or of a string wrapped around a stick.

In other, and probably later specimens we find that the rim has been somewhat flared, perhaps with the idea that the edge would thus be strengthened, and also to afford a means of holding the vessel by a cord around its neck. The next step was to make some simple decoration on the edge of the flared rim, either by impressing it with the wrapped stick, or with the edge of a shell, or by punching little depressions with the end of a sharpened bone.

These attempts led to further efforts at producing a stronger and more decorative rim, in which the natives of the Iroquois region appear to have set the fashion, producing pots with a thickened and deepened rim, which was sometimes formed into four angular ears, into which the neck of the pot was neatly flared. The rim now offered a space around the top of the vessel to which decorative effects could be effectively applied, and the form of decoration which the Iroquois developed was a geometric pattern of horizontal and diagonal lines scored in the clay, with very interesting and pleasing effects.

The rim in such vessels was sometimes gracefully curved between the four angular projections, and its edge was given a serrated form by pressing it with various objects, such as a snail-shell, or sometimes with the finger-nail of the potter-artist.

The natives of the New York City area had not proceeded far in this form of domestic art, when vessels which had been produced and decorated, in imitation of the superior shape and more elaborate design of the Iroquois, began to appear among their possessions.

When the Mohawk warriors invaded the region of New York City, and subjugated the Lenape they probably took many prisoners back to their home region. It was perhaps by returned prisoners that the methods, the implements, and the pottery designs of the Iroquois nation were brought to the Lenape.

The local potter began to imitate these characteristic ornaments, and thus produced a form of decorated vessel which is known as "Sub-Iroquoian," exhibiting the designs of the northern potters applied by local artists to vessels of local construction. The rims were thickened, and the neck was introduced, which led to a more graceful shape of the vessel.

The conspicuous feature of the Iroquois jar was the formation of the upper part of the rim into the four ears or angular projections of which mention has been made. The purpose of these ears may have been to support a cover over the contents of the vessel while cooking. When the rim between the ears was curved, the artistic appearance of the vessel was enhanced.

A beautiful and complete specimen of this form of vessel was found by W. L. Calver and this author at 214th Street, on the island of Manhattan.* This has four incised lines carried around the curved rim; between the projections and the face of the rim it is scored with vertical and angular lines, while the base of the rim just above the neck is marked by small incisions made with the

---

* Anthropological Papers, American Museum of Natural History, Vol. III, Plate XV.

SUB-IROQUOIS POTTERY JAR FROM CLAUSON POINT,
BRONX, NEW YORK. *PHOTOGRAPH BY ALANSON B. SKIN-
NER, 1918. COURTESY OF THE MUSEUM OF THE AMERICAN
INDIAN, HEYE FOUNDATION*

114a

A PARTLY COMPLETED CELT

MUSSEL-SHELL DECORATION

SNAIL-SHELL MARKINGS

A WAR ARROW

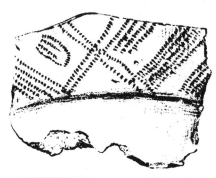

AN ATTEMPT AT IROQUOIAN DESIGN

POTTERY FROM THROG'S NECK

THESE FRAGMENTS CLEARLY SHOW THE EFFORTS MADE BY
THE ARTIST TO IMITATE DESIGNS UPON VESSELS MADE BY
THE IROQUOIS. SOME OF THE MARKINGS ARE EVIDENTLY
MADE FROM MEMORY, AS THEY ARE NOT DEFINITE ENOUGH
TO BE ACTUAL COPIES. THE LINES OF DEPRESSION WERE MADE
BY THE USE OF A STICK WRAPPED WITH A CORD.

114b

human finger-nail or with the shell of a snail, which makes a similar impression. The shape of the neck, the curve of the body, and its tapered base, are admirably proportioned.

The pot lay on its side, its lowest part being that in which a round hole had been formed, and the means of drainage of its interior being thus provided, it had kept dry during its long sojourn underground, and it was extracted in complete condition. It is now one of the exhibits at the American Museum of Natural History. Its burial in so shallow a pit, dug with evident haste in the sand hill where it was hidden, leads to the supposition that it was thus concealed by its owners when abandoning their homes in haste. It seems probable that the same occasion which caused the abandonment of another fine vessel found at 231st Street,* only a mile away, was that fatal panic which was brought about by the arrival on the Hudson of canoes with northern warriors, intent upon exacting tribute from our natives.

Doubtless such vessels would have proved welcome spoils to the aggressive tax collectors, but very unfortunate losses to the taxpayers. We may be justified in reconstructing the scene, as the unfortunate Rechgawawanc fled across the Inwood valley, loaded down with their household belongings, and doubtless burdened with helpless infants, stopping on the way to scrape out a hole in which the precious vessel was laid and covered over, to be recovered upon their expected return, which never occurred.

These circumstances fit in with that dreadful occasion (February 25, 1643) when the misguided Dutch slaughtered the refugees at Corlears Hook and at Paulus Hook, and Indian men, women, and children were ruthlessly stabbed and drowned.

The unfortunate natives of Kingsbridge evidently failed to return, or to recapture their household treasures, which were left in the position in which they were abandoned, to be found again after two centuries of concealment.

---

* Preserved in the Museum of the American Indian, Heye Foundation.

XXXII
BURIALS OF THE DEAD

THE disposal of the remains of the dead was a problem that was met by our natives in characteristic Indian fashion.

There is reason to suppose that some bodies were burned by fire, but many burials have been uncovered which were evidently placed in graves with particular care and in accordance with a well-defined system.

A characteristic feature is the position of the body, usually described as a seated attitude. This was, however, a rather misleading description, for many people have derived therefrom the idea that the body was placed upright in such a position as it would occupy in a chair or on a bench.

But the fact is that the remains were usually strained into a crouching attitude, and were bound with thongs in such manner as to occupy as little space as possible, the knees brought up under the chin, and the lower part of the legs strapped tight against the thighs. In this condition the body was laid upon its side in an oval-shaped excavation, which was scraped out by hand, by a stone, or by a large shell. Another theory which has widespread acceptance was to the effect that the body was laid in such a position that the face was directed towards the rising sun or in an easterly direction.

Many burials carefully examined are found to have been placed with no regard to the points of the compass.

We therefore find that our Indians of the region of the City of New York usually prepared a corpse for burial by compressing the limbs into the least possible space, and that the remains were then laid sidewise in the grave. All burials, however, were not arranged upon the same plan. A very recent discovery was made at Throg's Neck, of a human interment in which the body had been laid out in extended form, flat on its back, with the skull resting upon a flat stone. The remains were undoubtedly Indian, being placed in the shallow grave amid a number of shell-filled pits and fire pits.

In the New York City region, burials have been discovered in which oyster shells were packed around and over the corpse, the purpose of which practice seems to have been the protection of the remains from wild animals. It may be assumed that this system of protection had developed after many burials had been disturbed in that manner, and that therefore some interments were lost, and that those which have survived for our inspection were such as had been provided with this covering. The number of burials that have been found in the New York area are relatively few.

Burial places were often well-defined spaces, selected for the purpose by reason of their suitable soil and the natural drainage of the surface. Some of the places of burial of the dead were said to have been fenced round or planted with a hedge, and the graves covered or sheltered with mats, of which naturally no remains have been found.[†] These practices may be of later date, copied from European methods. Burials on village sites are found in haphazard positions, sometimes in an abandoned food pit, or below a fire pit.

The name of the dead person died with them. It was the practice always to avoid mentioning the name of the deceased in the presence of relatives.

Some burials which were uncovered at the village of Shora-kappok (Seaman Avenue, Inwood, Manhattan), were very carefully cleared, and close attention was given to details, which will justify a description.[‡]

[†] New York Historical Society, Vol. 1, p. 201.
[‡] The Indians of Manhattan Island, Skinner, Amer. Mus. of Natural History.

These burials were within the area of the village, close to numerous shell-pits. The remains consisted only of bones, and there were no evidences of objects such as vessels or ornaments.

The graves were shallow, about two and a half to three feet in depth, grubbed out of clear sand, oval in shape.

One skeleton was that of a female, whose forearms had been crossed over her breast, the hands at the neck. The legs were closely folded against the body. The remains lay on the right side, the face towards the south. In the region of the knees there was a considerable part of the bones of an infant, irregularly disposed, as if its body had been laid flat on the knees of the adult.

Between the ribs on the right side of the skeleton, there was a triangular arrow-head of black chert. The presence of this deadly missile opened the door to conjecture. The triangular arrow-point is usually attributed to Iroquoian ownership, and its presence in the unfortunate woman's body can point only to some bloodthirsty assault upon unprotected natives, when the attacking party shot down their victims regardless of sex and age.

Another and equally interesting burial was uncovered only about twenty feet south of the grave of the woman and child. In an oval space carefully covered by oyster shells, there lay the framework of a full grown male, closely folded, the left arm crossing the chest. The right arm, however, was extended in a very unusual manner, and piled upon it there was laid a number of human bones surmounted by a skull, the back of which had been broken in, leaving a ragged orifice about three inches long. When carefully cleaned and examined the ends of the arms and leg bones proved to be scorched and burnt. The skeleton was slight in size and afforded indications of having been that of a female.

Here, then, were the elements of another interesting series of conjectures. We have the young man, his age judged by his teeth being about thirty-five years. He dies, whether by disease or violence we cannot tell, but at the time of the burial, the remains of a female are interred with him. She had been killed, and her body partly roasted; then her frame had been taken apart with particular care, and the limbs carefully packed upon the right arm of the man, and the head set on top of the pile. It is natural to surmise that she was his squaw, and that for some reason she was killed at the time of his decease, and her remains after an attempt to dispose of them by fire were placed in the same grave.

A burial was discovered at the Snakapins village site in Clauson Point, below a large bed of ashes that had accumulated about the centre of the occupied site.

This situation may have been selected from the necessity of finding an excavation free from frost. The remains were those of a large male and lay on one side, doubled up, and at the knees there was a fine bone knife, and near by a bone awl or perforator. These objects seem to have been those which would have been utilized in the manufacture or repair of nets and may lead to the conjecture that the skeleton was that of the owner of the tools who might thus have been the netmaker of the village community.

Several burials were found at this place, and also at the Weir Creek village site in which a large boulder-stone had been placed on the skull. There were several burials within the area of the latter village, which had been placed in empty or partly emptied food-pits.

The descendants of the Lenape still entertain the belief that the spirit of mankind does not leave the dead body upon its decease, but lingers around the corpse for a period of eleven days, after which it departs, and passes through several stages of spiritual resorts to the twelfth heaven.

Indian burials were thus conducted in the imagined presence of the spirit of the deceased, and were often accompanied by demonstrations of affection and grief of extravagant character. While the men would restrain themselves in presence of the deceased, the women demonstrated their grief by beating their breasts, scratching their faces and calling upon the departed. If the occasion brought bereavement to a mother, she would cut off her hair, and it would

119

be burnt in the presence of the mourners. There are several historical references to the practice of building a fence around a grave. Harrington's enquiries confirmed this custom and his informants stated that a grave was always protected by a low fence of logs.

The system which was adopted seems to have been to place pieces of wood around the corpse and to cover the opening with other slabs of wood, on which soil and stones were thrown.

Around this grave posts were placed which gave the appearance of a little hut. It was considered a very reprehensible act to deface or injure any part of the structure.

XXXIII
ENTER THE WHITE MAN

With the arrival of the little ship, "The Half Moon," we reach the point in the life of the Indians of New York City where recorded facts take the place of unwritten history.

The vessel itself was an object of great local interest, but inasmuch as white men had been settled on the continent for many years, in Canada, in Virginia, and in Florida, as well as in New Mexico, it is assumable that the Lenape had heard of them, and that their character and their possession of superior tools and weapons, were already known to some extent to our local natives.

The appearance of European discoverers on the shores of America had occurred at intervals over a long period of time:

Leif Ericson and his brother Thorwald, not only visited but landed in New England, in 1001-2

Hundreds of years then elapsed before Columbus blundered into the West Indies, in 1492

He was followed by Ponce de Leon, who landed in Florida and took possession in the name of the Spanish Kingdom, in 1513

Giovanni Verrazano, with a French expedition, made his way probably as far as the outer Bay of New York, in 1524

Jacques Cartier sailed up the St. Lawrence and landed inland as far as Montreal, in 1534

Francisco Coronado headed an expedition from Mexico which penetrated the country as far as Santa Fe, in . . 1540

Tristan de Luca, with a Spanish expedition, was hunting
for gold in Georgia, in   1560
George Weymouth, exploring the Massachusetts coast,
treacherously seized and carried away five Indians, in   1605
John Smith and an English band landed and settled at
Jamestown, Virginia, in   1607
Samuel de Champlain was engaged in a fight between the
Hurons and Iroquois, in July   1609
Then came Henry Hudson and his crew in the "Half
Moon," who entered New York Bay, September . . .   1609

If our local Indians had any communication with other natives
resident either south or northeast along the coast, they might have
heard something of the people of a bleached or white race, who were
from time to time appearing out of the watery wilderness, and
would have been more or less prepared to expect the arrival of some
of the same kind of antagonistic and unscrupulous wayfarers. On
the other hand, the ship itself was an amazing novelty. Adriaen
Van der Donck, writing in 1656, said that many of the natives
living at that date (that is, more than forty years after the arrival
of Hudson's ship) had witnessed its appearance in the waters of
New York. They told him that they knew not what to think, but
stood in deep and solemn amazement, wondering whether it came
from heaven, while others had surmised that it might be a strange
fish or sea-monster.

The size of Hudson's ship no doubt appeared amazing to men
accustomed to a log canoe, but when part of the crew appeared
in a dinghy, they descended to a commonplace level, and venturing
as they did into the country of the belligerent Raritans, in the
Kill-van-Kull, it is no wonder that they became the target for
arrows, one of which struck and killed John Coleman, one of the
English sailors of the Half Moon.

The natives visiting the ship brought their canoes loaded with
various materials of their own production, which they offered to

ENTER THE WHITE MAN

THE ARRIVAL OF THE HALF MOON IN THE BAY OF NEW YORK WAS THE FIRST CLOSE
CONTACT OF THE WHITE AND RED RACES IN THE AREA OF THE CITY OF NEW YORK. THE
ORIGINAL VESSEL LONG AGO DISAPPEARED, BUT A COMPLETE REPRODUCTION, FROM ANCIENT
PLANS AND MODELS WAS CONSTRUCTED IN HOLLAND, AND WAS PRESENTED BY THE GOVERN-
MENT OF THE NETHERLANDS TO THE UNITED STATES OF AMERICA, UPON THE OCCASION
OF THE HUDSON-FULTON CELEBRATION IN 1909. FROM THIS REPLICA THE DRAWING IS MADE.

122a

122b

THE PURCHASE OF MANHATTAN ISLAND FROM THE INDIANS, 1626. OIL PAINTING ON PROCESSED CARDBOARD.
PHOTOGRAPH COURTESY OF THE MUSEUM OF THE CITY OF NEW YORK

the sailors hanging over the bulwarks, in exchange for almost any object that excited their cupidity. These products included maize, just at that time in the harvesting, and the produce of the forest in the shape of "currants," or wild grapes.

They brought green tobacco, which they had grown, and hemp, probably in the form of the thread or cord with which they made their nets. They were loosely dressed, Juet wrote, in deer-skins. Some wore mantles of feathers, and some were covered with good furs of bear, deer, beaver, racoon, mink and wild cat, which excited the interest of the newcomers, and doubtless originated the suggestion which led Hudson to the belief that a profitable business could be developed in furs, which afterwards proved to be the case.

Robert Juet, mate of Henry Hudson, wrote down in his story of the voyage to New York his impressions, which are the first written description of the natives of the area of the greater City:

"The people of the countrey came aboard of us, seeming very glad of our comming, and brought greene tobacco, and gave us of it for knives and beads. They goe in deere skins loose, well dressed. They have yellow copper. They desire cloathes, and are very civill. They have great store of maize, or Indian wheate, whereof they make good bread. The countrey is full of great and tall oaks.

"Our men went on land there, and saw great store of men, women, and children, who gave them tabacco at their comming on land.

"So they went up into the woods, and saw great store of very goodly oakes and some currants. One of them came aboard and brought some dryed, and gave me some, which were sweet and good.

"This day many of the people came aboard, some in mantles of feathers, and some in skinnes of divers sorts of good furres. Some women also came to us with hempe. They had red copper tabacco pipes, and other things of copper they did weare about their neckes. At night they went on land again."

The description of the natives of New York thus entered in the record of this voyage, was of informative interest, but we may bear in mind that the observers were not ethnologists, nor were they experienced in psychology. Their observations, therefore, must be received as those of rough and ill-educated sailors, and we may also remember that they were wholly unacquainted with the language of the natives.

Some copper objects have been found on Indian sites in or near the City, notably at Hewletts, on Long Island. A copper object came to light from an excavation at the site of the Brooklyn Bridge. But copper was certainly a very unpromising and even undesirable material for a tobacco pipe. We may assume, therefore, that the reddish pottery pipes of the natives were mistaken for copper, but there is evidence that some of the ornaments worn round their necks were of that metal in the form of beads. The remains of a child buried at Tottenville, Staten Island, had a string of copper beads around the neck.

Some years later De Laet described their use of "stone pipes for smoking tobacco," and Juet described the pottery vessels of the natives as "pots of earthe to dresse their meats in." These were not very exact descriptions, but are a little closer to fact than the red copper pipes.

A second visit of the "Half Moon" was designed to secure a supply of the coveted furs, which were then in great demand in Europe, and for which good prices could be obtained in Holland. The voyage was successful. For mere trinkets the crew obtained a cargo of valuable skins, and the Indians were found to be ready traders. Their friendly willingness to trade was proclaimed to the public in Holland as an incentive for further ventures.

In 1611, Christiaensen found his way to New York Bay, and on his return to Holland, he struck up a partnership with Adriaen Block, with whom he visited the Hudson River, obtained a cargo of furs, and induced or kidnapped a couple of young natives, who were dubbed "Valentine and Orson," to visit Europe. Valentine and Orson is an old-time romance that even in those days was ancient. It was the story of twin brothers, born in vastly differing circumstances, and was first printed in 1489, and in England in 1550.

The glowing reports of these traders and the appearance of the young visitors aroused the interest of merchants in possession of capital, who engaged in the business, and sent several vessels to Manhattan. Their long-boats traversed the interior waterways, visiting Indian stations and trading trinkets and perhaps more useful articles for the coveted skins and furs. The supply in our fishing villages was probably soon exhausted, and the skins were sought in surrounding territory, where the hardy traders proceeded along the Indian pathways to remote settlements.

Their vessel, "The Tiger," anchored off the Kapsee Rocks at Manhattan, took fire one night, and thus brought about the first white man's settlement upon the future center of the City of New York. The nearby natives proved practical friends to the ship-wrecked men, providing them with food and no doubt helping them to build the huts in which they found shelter on the end of Man-hattan Island, the site of which has been supposed to be that slight elevation overlooking the Mahikanittuk which is now occupied by Number 39 Broadway. Nearby they built another vessel in which they made their way back to Europe.

There is on record, in the "Breeden Raedt" record, a statement by the natives that "when the Dutch lost a ship, we provided the white men with food until the new ship was finished."

This temporary occupation was followed by the arrival of a number of immigrants, Walloon religious refugees, who took up a residence on the lower end of the island, and eked out a living by trading for skins with the natives and bartering with the crews of ships that arrived from Europe.

XXXIV
THE PURCHASE OF MANHATTAN

THIS transaction has become famous, has been referred to by many writers, and has been illustrated by various imaginative artists until the circumstances have been distorted.

The affair is commonly represented as an arrival of Dutch immigrants upon the shore, and their offering to a group of natives (who are neatly dressed and are armed with bows, arrows and spears), a chestful of articles of clothing and bric-a-brac, in one illustration even including books and a crucifix. We shall examine the circumstances and endeavor to record a correct picture of the momentous event.

At the period of the transaction, there were already resident upon the island the group previously mentioned, comprising thirty families of Walloon settlers, refugees from religious persecution in Flanders, who had been squatters on the island in hovels of native form for many years. They had evidently lived on good terms with the nearby natives, who must have provided them with food, and perhaps traded their farm products and the skins of wild animals for the poor Walloons' trinkets or clothing. This early settlement was the underlying cause of the decision in Holland, by which the Dutch West India Company was empowered to effect a colonization of the New Netherland region, which included the area of the present City of New York.

In pursuance of this policy, and in view of the poverty, sickness and ignorance of the Walloon settlers, the Company sent in 1624, two "Kranken-besoeckers," or Comforters of the Sick, one of whom was Jan Huyck, appointed as custodian of the communal stores. His young wife was a sister of Peter Minuit, who later became the Governor of the colonists.

The situation in regard to the natives was that their occupation of the island of Manhattan was divided between the members of two chieftaincies, the Canarsee occupying the southern end, and the Weckquaesgeek, the upper or northern part, the division between the two being the rather unattractive because uncultivable region now comprised in the forties and fifties of our modern street system, which was then probably covered with scrub forest and infested with wolves, wildcats and snakes.

When Peter Minuit was sent out to act as a governor of the shabby little colony, he must have landed and assumed his duties before the question of a title to the site of the settlement became sufficiently important to require a purchase of the land from the natives occupying the island.

The colonists do not appear to have made themselves acquainted with the native situation, nor with the division of the island by native occupation, so that when the negotiation for a payment for the territory occupied by the colony was begun, it was taken up with the nearby Canarsee, whose wily leaders conveyed the impression of their ownership of the whole island, and thus secured for themselves and their own people all the goods which the white men were offering.

The home of the neighboring natives seems to have been at the Collect Pond, north of which they had reclaimed a tract of cultivated land, known as "Werpoes." This planting ground was of vital importance to the colonists whose homes had been established on the rocky and uncultivable southern point of Manhattan. The only tract in that locality offering any opportunity for cultivation was the area which is now our City Hall Park. This was probably also a small planting field of the natives, if one may judge by the

127

presence of oyster shells in the soil, and the sharp bend of the path around the space.

However that may be, the natives came to an understanding that for certain gifts of goods they would vacate their home at Werpoes and allow the white settlers the full use of the island. The famous transaction then took place, presumably at or near the white men's headquarters, where there was by that time a stone storehouse in which their surplus goods and store of furs was housed under the care of Jan Huyck. We are somewhat misled by the monetary value of twenty-four dollars, or rather of sixty Dutch guilders, which was placed upon the goods thus offered to the natives, but we may remember that coinage meant nothing to those people. The goods which they obtained assumed only such value to them as was commensurate with what they were asked to concede. They were doubtless knives, axes, hoes and some clothing. Perhaps a keg of rum was included.

The natives of the village at that period were led by a sachem of the name of Meijeterma, and the leading sachem of the chieftaincy of the Canarsee enjoyed the name of Seyseys. These were the principals in the transaction.

The inhabitants of Werpoes moved over to Brooklyn, where they found a new home at a place called Nayack, near Fort Hamilton. We also find another village of the name of "Worpos," situated at Hoyt and Baltic Streets in Brooklyn, which may have been established and named by some of those who moved away from the village on Manhattan.

The only contemporary account of that momentous transaction is contained in a letter written by a Dutch official, which was dated November the fifth, in the year 1626, and reported news from New Netherland by the good ship "The Arms of Amsterdam," which sailed out of our Bay, September 23rd of that year. It runs:

> "Our people there are of good courage, and live peaceably. Their women have borne children there, they have bought the island of Manhattes from the Wild men for the value of sixty guilders."

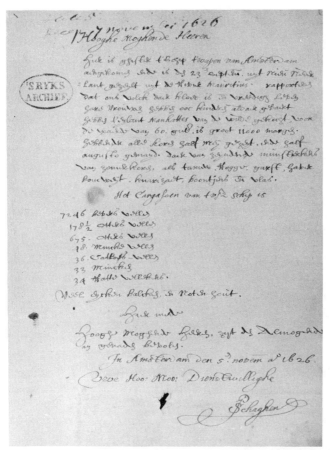

THE ONLY RECORDED DOCUMENT OF THE ORIGINAL PURCHASE OF
MANHATTAN, THIS LETTER WAS WRITTEN IN AMSTERDAM, NOVEMBER
5, 1626, BY PIETER JANSEN SCHAGHEN, A DEPUTY TO THE STATES-
GENERAL AT THE HAGUE. TRANSLATED, IT READS:

HIGH MIGHTY SIRS:

HERE ARRIVED YESTERDAY THE SHIP THE ARMS OF AMSTERDAM
WHICH SAILED FROM NEW NETHERLAND OUT OF THE MAURITIUS
(HUDSON) RIVER ON SEPTEMBER 23; THEY REPORT THAT OUR
PEOPLE THERE ARE OF GOOD COURAGE, AND LIVE PEACEABLY.
THEIR WOMEN, ALSO, HAVE BORNE CHILDREN THERE, THEY HAVE
BOUGHT THE ISLAND MANHATTES FROM THE WILD MEN FOR THE
VALUE OF SIXTY GUILDERS. THEY SOWED ALL THEIR GRAIN IN
THE MIDDLE OF MAY, AND HARVESTED IT IN THE MIDDLE OF
AUGUST. THEREOF SAMPLES OF SUMMER GRAIN, SUCH AS WHEAT,
RYE, BARLEY, OATS, BUCKWHEAT, CANARY SEED, SMALL BEANS,
AND FLAX. THE CARGO OF THE AFORESAID SHIP IS: 7246 BEAVER
SKINS, 178½ OTTER (HALF-OTTER?) SKINS, 36 WILD-CAT SKINS,
33 MINK, 34 RAT SKINS. MANY LOGS OF OAK AND NUT-WOOD.
HEREWITH BE YE HIGH MIGHTY SIRS, COMMENDED TO THE
ALMIGHTY'S GRACE, IN AMSTERDAM, NOVEMBER 5, ANNO 1626.
YOUR HIGH MIGHT'S OBEDIENT,
P. SCHAGHEN

128a

128b

SIGNING THE TREATY WITH THE WECKQUAESGEEK INDIANS. JONAS BRONCK. 1642
PHOTOGRAPH COURTESY OF THE MUSEUM OF THE CITY OF NEW YORK

Catalina Trico, one of the women referred to, had come to New York with the ship "Unity" in 1623, with four other women. All of the women were married while on the voyage, and settled with their spouses on the south end of Manhattan Island. By the date of this transaction, there were thirty-two families squatted upon the island, most of them being Walloon or Flemish refugees, who had found asylum at Leyden, where they had been neighbors of those English refugees who made their way to Massachusetts, and with whom we are acquainted as "the Pilgrims."

Relying upon the validity and scope of the purchase, various hardy pioneers made their way to the upper end of the island, which presented natural features that were highly attractive, such as the wide marshes of Harlem, the wooded ridge of Washington Heights, and extensive fishing opportunities along the irregular shores of the Inwood district. Here, however, they found the natives of another chieftaincy, the Weckquaesgeek, resident in places which had been occupied by them and their predecessors for a long period of time, who were very tenacious as to their ownership of the territory, and were naturally quite unwilling to abandon their sheltered homes, their rich planting fields, their choice fishing grounds, and the graves of their ancestors.

The source of the conflicts that took place between these natives and the Harlem settlers, the blood that was shed and the property that was destroyed may be found in the ill-managed and misunderstood bargain for the purchase of Manhattan.

Certain Sachems of the Indians met the British Governor Lovelace in 1670 to arrange for the sale of Staten Island. At this interview some of the natives present "laid claim to the land by Harlem," thus maintaining the assertion of their ownership of the upper part of Manhattan Island. On this occasion they were confronted with Minuit's purchase of 1626, the deed showing "it was bought and paid for," but the natives were not satisfied, and renewed their claim later.

XXXV
INDIAN SETTLEMENTS IN THE AREA
NOW OCCUPIED BY NEW YORK CITY

In the following pages, there will be found a list of all the places within the area of the City, which are known to have been occupied by Indians. These are numbered, using the same numeration as that which was applied to them in "Indian Paths in the Great Metropolis." The sites are also marked upon a map of each borough, so that the reader may observe the situation of the native settlements.

It is interesting to observe from these maps that the majority of the native villages were situated on the shores of the waters of New York. This confirms the opinion, derived from a study of their ways and habits, that they were largely engaged in fishing, which occupation afforded their chief source of food. Only a relatively small number of villages or stations were located in the interior country.

The situation of a dwelling-place also appears naturally to have been mainly dependent upon a nearby source of potable water, which is a primary necessity in human existence. In the work of exploration, it has been found that it is profitable to investigate the ground near a spring or brook for signs of Indian occupancy, while, inversely, it is a waste of time to explore land on which there is no running water or spring, or which is remote from some such source of drinking-water.

The position of a permanent village often seems to have been selected with care and with a purpose. A sandy soil and a moderate grade of the surface afforded a natural drainage, and the shelter afforded by forest or by a hill was desirable as some protection against too inquisitive visitors. The same advantages were sought by white settlers. The site of some early dwellings has been found to be that of an Indian village, and the Indian planting-ground seems to have been frequently the beginning of the settler's clearing and farmed land.

There is good reason to believe that the natives were of much benefit to settlers who were destitute of food and shelter, not only by providing shelter and food, but by teaching them or by permitting them to learn their methods of cultivation, and by pointing out the most productive soil.

The pathways which led from the lodges of the natives were certainly the first means of communication with the interior of the country; and in many cases they have decided the course of our present highways.

The sites of Indian homes within the Greater City are now lost beneath the network of buildings in our modern city, and the overwhelming tide of modern construction, so that the record of their one-time position assumes a value that may be the more appreciated as time proceeds.

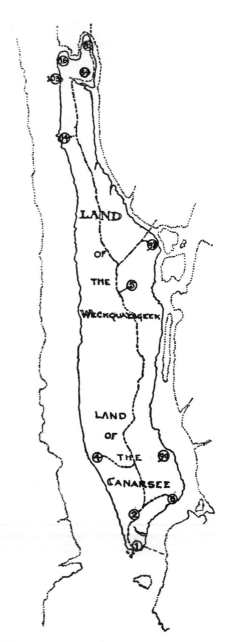

INDIAN SITES IN THE BOROUGH OF MANHATTAN

INDIAN SITES IN THE BOROUGH OF MANHATTAN

(The numbers are those appearing upon the accompanying map)

I. KAPSEE

The southern extremity of the island of Manhattan, the name being probably applied also to the rocks in the tideway which are now buried under Battery Park.

Abundant shells on the East shore line, now Pearl Street, testified to native use of the vicinity of the shore, probably as a landing place for canoes.

2. WERPOES

A native village site, situated on the line of Elm Street, between Duane Street and Worth Street. Masses of shells were disturbed on grading Pearl Street through this site.

3. RECHTANCK

This was a village situated on Corlears Hook, probably near a supply of fresh water, which ran in a little brook to the East River, at Jefferson, Henry, Clinton and Madison Streets, facing south on the East River.

This village was the scene of the massacre of the natives by Dutch soldiery on the night of February 25, 1643.

4. SAPOHANIKAN

A place of trade on the shore of the Hudson River, between Bethune and Horatio Streets in Greenwich Village. Its name indicates that there was a plantation of tobacco, but there does not appear to have been any source of fresh water, and therefore it would not have been a permanent settlement or village.

99. SHEPMOES

A settlement or station which seems to have been situated on a small tract of upland rising from the marshes near the East River, between East Twelfth and East Thirteenth Streets, at Avenue C.

5. KONAANDE KONGH

This was the home of Rechewac, a chief who resided in the vicinity known as Rechewanis, indicating a "little sandy stream." The name of the native village which was his headquarters seems to have been KONAANDE KONGH. (See History of Harlem, Riker 1881, p. 287). Its situation was about Park Avenue at 94th Street.

98. SCHORRAKIN

A fishing camp, on which many stone points were found, is mentioned in the "History of Harlem" by James Riker. It was situated on the bank of the East River at 119th Street.

84. MUSCOOTA

A name applied to the low land which afterwards became the property of the Dyckman and Nagel families and is now covered with apartment houses extending between Dyckman Street on the south, and the Ship Canal on the north. The name applied also to the contiguous waterway, or Harlem River. In this locality there were several places occupied by the natives, and in the approximate centre of the tract there was a ceremonial site on 212th Street, between Tenth Avenue and Broadway. At this place there were several pits in which were burials, one of a dog, another of a turtle, and another contained the fishbones which seem to have formed a breast ornament. For additional details regarding this site and others, see "Washington Heights, Its Eventful Past," by Reginald Pelham Bolton.

103. DYCKMAN STREET at HUDSON RIVER

This was evidently a very ancient site, for there was a deeply buried deposit of shells and ashes beneath which were crude stone implements, the bones of bears, and the horns of elk. The deposit was on the south side of Dyckman Street near the Hudson close to the "Little Sand Bay," which is now filled in. Staff Street has been constructed on its southerly boundary.

134

14. FORT WASHINGTON PARK
Known as Jeffrey's Hook or Juffrouw's Hoek

This was a fishing station used by the natives, for on and around the little beaches at the Point there are masses of shells and wood ashes, and a number of small arrow-points have been found among the rocks, which were probably lost in shooting or spearing fish.

16. SHORAKAPPOK

This was an Indian name, which was applied to both the waterway and to the contiguous land situated at the extreme northern part of the island of Manhattan, now known as Inwood and Inwood Hill Park. The principal native settlement seems to have been situated along the line of Seaman Avenue, north of Dyckman Street, and it extended into the woodlands which now compose Inwood Hill Park. The village site included many food pits filled with shells, several burials of human beings, and also those of dogs, many stone objects, and masses of shells, ashes and carbonized materials.

A cave and rockshelters used by the natives can still be seen in Inwood Hill Park, and many fireplaces have been uncovered there by the Museum of the American Indian, Heye Foundation. Many stone objects and broken pottery left by the native residents can be seen in the Cottage at the Great Tree which is maintained by Dyckman Institute.

85. MARBLE HILL

Scattered shells and objects indicate the presence of natives at or near the place when the stream could be crossed, at the Wading Place, which were probably left by natives waiting fall of the tide.

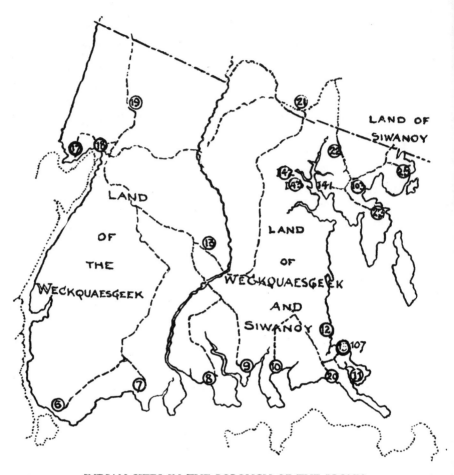

INDIAN SITES IN THE BOROUGH OF THE BRONX

INDIAN SITES IN THE BOROUGH OF THE BRONX

(The numbers are those which appear on the accompanying map)

6. RANACHQUA

The tract of land, about 500 acres in extent, situated in Morrisania, which was purchased in 1639 by Jonas Bronck. The occupied site of a native village seems to have been at Cypress Avenue, near 131st Street, where food-pits and Indian implements have been found.

7. QUINNAHUNG

Hunt's Point, or the Great Planting Neck, on which several native sites have been located:

1. At site of the Richardson dwelling, and near the Hunt Burying Ground.
2. On the Dickey estate at Randall Avenue, close to the Hunt's Point Road.
3. On a mound in the marsh land, now filled-in on the line of Eastern Boulevard.
4. At the end of the Point, where the old Hunt house used to stand, now lost in the gas-works.

10. BROCKETT'S NECK
BURIAL POINT
ZEREGA'S NECK
OR
OLD FERRY POINT

An Indian station, probably a fishing camp, is indicated by shells scattered over a space alongside the Old Ferry Road, and near the shoreline, but careful search has failed to afford evidence of a native village. We found a small spring close to the east shore, in and near which were some small fragments of pottery and other Indian objects, which indicated that the place had been used as a fishing camp.

8. SNAKAPINS

A native village on Sound View Avenue, at Leland Avenue and Lacombe Avenue, where about sixty food-pits were uncovered, with human burials and many other indications of native occupancy, by Alanson Skinner.

See publications of the Museum of the American Indian, Heye Foundation, 1919, Vol. V, No. 4.

9. CASTLE POINT OR CASTLE HILL

A native station, situated on the elevated ground, on the west bank of Westchester Creek, once the site of the residence of the Screven family. There was evidently a planting-field in the low ground extending from this eminence, on which we found several Indian stone implements. Castle Point Avenue extends to the end of the point, where masses of clam and oyster shells were accumulated, some of the shells being bored for the material for beads.

The point is now covered by boat yards.

20. THROG'S NECK

There was a very extensive native settlement at the end of East Tremont Avenue along Schurz Avenue, which at the time of this writing is still under exploration. It occupied a space of about a quarter of a mile in length and centered upon the little beach about 300 feet east of the Collis Huntington house. The beach used to be reached by an old lane which may have been the successor of an Indian pathway. Many food-pits, several fireplaces, some human burials and much broken pottery and stone artifacts, point to long occupancy of this place which was in territory controlled by Indians of the Siwanoy tribe, but utilized also by the Weckquaesgeek. This site has not yet been completely explored, but is under observation by the Museum of the American Indian, Heye Foundation.

138

ROCK SHELTERS

ANY FORM OF SHELTER THAT NATURE PROVIDED WAS UTILIZED BY THE INDIAN. AN
VERHANGING ROCK OFFERED AN OPPORTUNITY OF SECURING A ROOF, AND THE OPEN SIDE
ULD BE CLOSED BY POLES FORMING A FRAME ON WHICH SKINS, OR SHEETS OF BARK COULD
SECURED MAKING A MORE OR LESS WEATHER PROOF WALL. THERE ARE SUCH ROCK-
ELTERS IN EXISTENCE THAT GIVE EVIDENCE OF HAVING BEEN UTILIZED IN THAT MANNER.
E SHELTER WHICH IS ILLUSTRATED IS ONE WHICH IS SITUATED IN INWOOD HILL PARK,
N THE ISLAND OF MANHATTAN. BENEATH ITS OVERHANGING ROOF THERE WAS A WOOD
RE, AND MANY ASHES SCATTERED AROUND IT.

138a

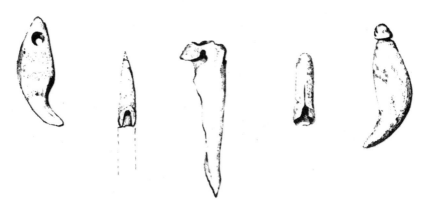

OBJECTS LEFT BY THE PRE-HISTORIC INDIANS AT WEIR CREEK STATION
BOROUGH OF THE BRONX

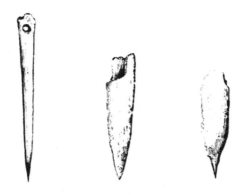

BONE IMPLEMENTS

SOME OF THESE HUMBLE FRAGMENTS ARE OF GREAT IMPORTANCE, AS THEY INDICAT
THE USE OF BONE AND HORN DURING A PERIOD OF TIME, BEFORE THE USE OF STONE AN
FLINT HAD DEVELOPED. IN THE LOWER LAYERS OF WASTE MATERIALS AT THE ANCIEN
INDIAN VILLAGE AT WEIR CREEK, EASTCHESTER BAY, BOROUGH OF THE BRONX, THES
OBJECTS WERE FOUND, NOT ACCOMPANIED BY ANY STONE TOOLS. UPPER LAYERS CONTAINE
FAMILIAR STONE IMPLEMENTS.

THE BEAR'S TEETH, PERFORATED OR GROUND FOR A FASTENING MAY HAVE BEEN HUN
AROUND THE NECK OF A HUNTER AS AN AMULET, OR TO HAVE THEM HANDY FOR USE I
SHAPING STONE TOOLS.

THE USE OF BONE POINTS FOR PERFORATING SKINS ILLUSTRATES THE CLUMSY METHO
OF ABORIGINAL STITCHING OF SKINS. THE BONE NEEDLE WITH A PERFORATION FOR A THREA
WAS FOUND IN THE UPPER PART OF A SHELL-PIT AT SEAMAN AVENUE. IT SEEMS PROBABL
THAT IT WAS MADE AFTER THE NATIVES HAD SEEN A EUROPEAN NEEDLE MADE WITH A
EYE. HUNDREDS OF YEARS PROBABLY ELAPSED BETWEEN THE MAKING OF THE BONE PE
FORATOR AND THE NEEDLE.

ARROWS WERE SOMETIMES TIPPED WITH THE SHARP POINT OF THE ANTLERS OF DEE
PROBABLY FASTENED TO THE WOODEN SHAFT BY RESIN.

138b

11. LOCUST POINT
on THROG'S NECK

A fishing camp with slight indications of occupancy.

12. WEIR CREEK

An important and extensive site is situated at Schley Avenue, on the shore of Eastchester Bay, in the vicinity of Throg's Neck. It gave evidences of occupation by aboriginal inhabitants who had not acquired the use of stone implements. It was explored by the late Alanson Skinner, surveyed by the writer, and is fully described in a publication of the Museum of the American Indian, Heye Foundation, Vol. V, No. 4.

13. BEAR SWAMP ROAD

An Indian settlement was situated on a brook close to the road. Robert Bolton asserts that it was the last which was occupied by the natives in the East Bronx district. It has not been explored, but evidences of its existence have been seen in gardens and picked up in vacant lots near the Bear Swamp Road at Downings Brook. See History of the County of Westchester. Robert Bolton, Vol. II, p. 264.

18. PAPARINEMIN
NOW
KINGSBRIDGE

This name was applied both to the tidal stream in which two tides used to rise and fall daily, and also to the island extending from 225th Street, nearly to 240th Street. At 231st Street there was an Indian settlement, perched on high ground overlooking the crossing of the path from the island to Kingsbridge, exactly in the centre of 231st Street. There were traces of other occupied places of small extent on the island, which may have been temporary in character.

17. NIPINICHSEN
BERRIANS NECK
SPUYTEN DUYVIL HILL
RIVERDALE

This is said to have been the site of a palisaded station or fortification, the precise situation of which is not known. There was much Indian debris of shells and ashes on the line of 231st Street, back of Ewen Park, near which there was a strong spring of good drinking water. The crest of the hill near the Henry Hudson monument was a good lookout point, commanding a view up and down the river, and nearby, on the estate of the late W. C. Muschenheim, a food-pit was discovered. We may conclude that the place was intended to be occupied only in times of danger. Its situation was very much exposed to wind and storm.

107. ADEE POINT
ON THROG'S NECK

Directly south across the mouth of Weir Creek is a site now covered with small dwellings. It was probably of the same general character as the Weir Creek site for which see Number 12.

23. ANN'S HOOK
ANHOEK
RODMAN'S NECK

On the shore of Pelham Bay, are extensive masses of shells and ashes which were explored by M. R. Harrington for the American Museum of Natural History. He found many evidences of Indian existence there. Bolton, in his "History of Westchester County, Vol. II, p. 36, relates the discovery of human burials there. Pelham waters teemed with fish, and attracted many natives from Manhattan during the summer seasons.

19. MOSHOLU or KESKESKICK
VAN CORTLANDT PARK

This was an extensive and probably permanent village, the traces of which were found around the Van Cortlandt Mansion and scattered over the playing-field adjoining the old building. The late J. B. James found there many traces of Indian occupation, food-pits, human burials and dog-burials, and he recovered and preserved pottery and stone artifacts.

103. LAAPHAWACHING
BARTOW ESTATE
PELL MANOR

The site of a considerable village on the Bartow estate was explored by Rev. W. Blackie, for the Museum of the American Indian, Heye Foundation. He found about twenty food-pits, in one of which there was a dog burial, and other indications of native existence.

The site is on the rising ground, on the north side of the driveway from the "Shore Road" to the Bartow mansion. It has been recently re-examined and is found to extend further towards the Sound. It was the home of those Siwanoy natives who sold the large tract comprising Pelham and New Rochelle, to Thomas Pell. South of the village the large oak tree was situated, which tradition identifies as the "Treaty Oak," beneath which the natives consummated the bargain with Pell.

21. EASTCHESTER

This once important place is now swallowed up in modern Mount Vernon. There are traces of an Indian settlement on the old Kingsbridge Road close to the Railroad Station of the Boston and Westchester Railway.

Bolton, in the "History of the County of Westchester," locates an Indian village on the Drake estate, the traces of which have not been found. There were many shells in a small sheltered piece of ploughed land, at Sixth Street, Mount Vernon.

22. THE SPLIT ROCK

This conspicuous and unusual natural object must have attracted the attention of the vigilant natives. There are nearby some slight traces of native occupancy, enough to justify the assumption that the place was visited, but was not permanently occupied by them.

This rock was long supposed to have been close to the site of the home of Anne Hutchinson, murdered by natives in 1643, but later investigations have decided that her home was across the Hutchinson River in Eastchester.*

141. HUTCHINSON RIVER

A point of land in Pelham Bay Park overlooking the river is covered with many shells, ashes and carbonized materials. It has the appearance of a fishing station.

25. HUNTERS ISLAND
MISHOW

This island is just within the boundary of the City of New York, and forms part of Pelham Bay Park. There are several places on the twin island where evidences of Indian occupancy can be seen. The shores yielded a number of specimens of stone implements, arrows and scrapers.

There is a large boulder or rock on the shore, which is supposed to have been the ceremonial stone known as "Mishow."

142. BAYCHESTER AVENUE
VREDELAND
LAND OF PEACE

Indian occupancy of a site at the mouth of Hutchinson Brook is evidenced by buried shells and ashes. The brook emerges from the upland into the marshes known as Hutchinson's Meadows. Explored by the writer and W. L. Calver.

* See "Woman Misunderstood." R. P. Bolton, 1932.

143. THE PRICKLY PEAR
PINCKNEY'S HUMACK

A rock island in Hutchinson's Meadows, about 400 feet east of Baychester Avenue, on which masses of shells and ashes have been left by native occupants. Some fragments of Indian pottery and part of a very small bowl confirm the use of the place, probably as a fishing camp.

PINCKNEY'S HUMACK, OR THE PRICKLY PEAR

THIS NAME WAS APPLIED, BY THE SETTLERS UPON THE EASTCHESTER PLANTING GROUND, O THE HUMMOCK OR ISLAND OF ROCK ON PHILIP PINCKNEY'S ALLOTMENT OF MEADOW AND. THE ROCK STANDS UP IN THE MARSHES THAT ARE STILL KNOWN BY THE NAME OF HE UNFORTUNATE ANNE HUTCHINSON. IN THE FOREGROUND IS HUTCHINSON'S BROOK, NOWN ALSO AS "BLACK DOG BROOK."
THE HUMMOCK WAS OCCUPIED BY INDIANS, PROBABLY AS A FISHING CAMP. IN THE ADDLE-SHAPED SPACE BETWEEN THE ROCKS, THERE IS A MASS OF OYSTER SHELLS AND OOD ASHES AND HIGHER UP IN THE CREVICE BETWEEN THE SLOPING ROCKS THERE WAS NOTHER COLLECTION OF WASTE MATERIALS. WE FOUND FRAGMENTS OF A VERY SMALL OTTERY CUP, ABOUT THREE INCHES HIGH, WHICH LOOKS LIKE A CHILD'S PLAYTHING.
IT SEEMS MOST PROBABLE THAT THE HUTCHINSON HOUSE WAS SITUATED NOT FAR ESTWARD OF THESE ROCKS, AND THESE NATIVES WERE HER CLOSE NEIGHBORS, AND MAY AVE TAKEN PART IN HER MURDER IN 1643.

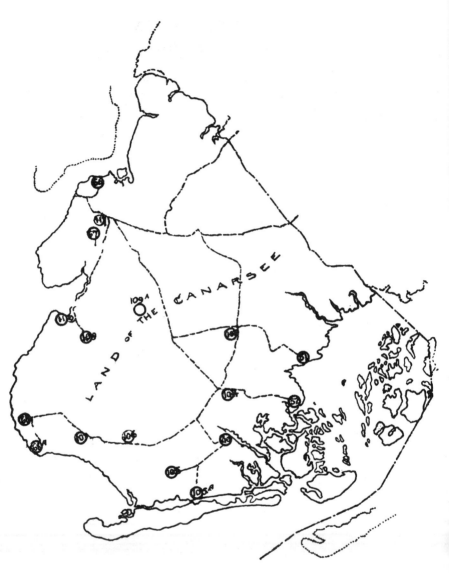

INDIAN SITES IN THE BOROUGH OF BROOKLYN

INDIAN SITES IN KINGS COUNTY

(The numbers are those which appear on the accompanying map)

66. RINNEGOKONCK

At Bridge Street, a site evidenced by waste materials, fire pits and implements described by Furman in "Antiquities of Long Island."

67. WERPOS

At Hoyt and Baltic Streets, Brooklyn, there was once a site having the same name as the village on Manhattan Island which was abandoned by the natives upon the sale of that island, and this place may have been in part their refuge. (See Number 68.)

117. MARECHAWIK

Supposed to have been an important village, in which the local sachem made his home, situated at Gallatin Place and Elm Place, Brooklyn. (See Colonial Documents of New York, Vol. XIV.)

110. GOWANUS BAY

There was an Indian station, marked by extensive shell beds, at 37th Street, near Third Avenue.

109A. SAND HILL

A sand hill, with buried pottery, arrowheads and broken clay pipes was uncovered in 1826, and is described by Furman in "Antiquities of Long Island."

109. SUNSET PARK

Around Benny-water Pond in Sunset Park, an old Indian site existed, extending to 37th Street near Sixth Avenue. See the Journal of Sluyter and Dankers.

108. MUSKYTTEHOOL

A site at Bedford Creek, or Paardegat, at the crossing of the Flatlands Road, is referred to as a "boundary place."

51. CANARSIE or CANARSEE

A village site, and extensive planting field, extended back from Canarsie Beach Park as far as Avenue J, centred on East 92nd Street.

52. WINNIPAGUE
BERGEN BEACH

There are extensive shell beds on this island, and stone implements have been found there. Its favorable situation indicates an important station of the Canarsee chieftaincy.

104. KESKAECHQUEREN
KNOWN TO THE DUTCH AS
AMERSFOORT
AND NOW
FLATLANDS

An important settlement at this place on which the paths converged, was a place of meeting and conference. There was also a burying-ground, and its location and the paths connecting it with other places indicate a place of considerable importance to the Canarsee and perhaps other chieftaincies. (See Colonial Documents, Vol. XIV.)

50. SHANSCOMACOCKE
GERRITSEN BASIN
RYDERS POINT

A native village existed here, indicated by many stone implements which were plowed up on the Ryder farm and are preserved in the Ryder homestead nearby. Burials were disturbed in the opening of Avenue U.

105. MASSABARKEM now GRAVESEND

A scattered settlement, in which old Lady Deborah Moody and her refugees from New England planted themselves. (Munsell, History of Kings County.)

105A. NARRIOCK
SHEEPSHEAD BAY

On the shores, shell-beds and debris indicate native occupancy—probably a fishing station.

106. THE INDIAN POND
MARLBORO

This Pond contained fresh water, always an attraction to the natives, and in its vicinity they had planting fields of considerable extent. The Pond lay close to the Mechawanienck or "Ancient Path."

107. NEW UTRECHT

A probable site, but not explored, through which there was probably a native trail leading to Gravesend Bay.

68. NAYACK
THE NARROWS

This is supposed to have been the place to which the natives of Werpoes removed after the sale of Manhattan Island. (See Indian Paths in the Great Metropolis, Bolton.) Furman relates that in 1837 a large collection or "cache" of flint blades was found there.

68A. FORT HAMILTON

Shell beds indicated occupation, probably as a fishing camp.

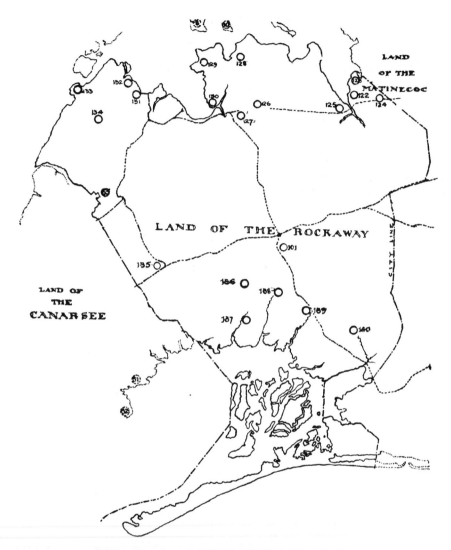

INDIAN SITES IN THE BOROUGH OF QUEENS

148

INDIAN SITES IN THE BOROUGH OF QUEENS

(The numbers are those which appear on the accompanying map)

101. JAMAICA or YAMECO

A native settlement, probably of very ancient occupancy. Since the name is derived from the Beaver, the site of the station may have been near a pond which was the home of those industrious animals. The site is said to have been situated on a creek, a mile south of Jamaica. (Thompson, B. F., History of Long Island, 1839.)

127. FLUSHING

A site with burials, of which eleven were uncovered in 1841. (See Furman, G., Antiquities of Long Island, 1875.)

126. FLUSHING (EAST)

Another site, with burials, was situated a mile east of Flushing, on which stone implements were found in 1880.

125. BAYSIDE

A site near Little Neck Bay, so far unexplored.

122. DOUGLASTON

A village settlement near Little Neck, on high ground overlooking Little Neck Bay, which may offer an opportunity for careful investigation.

123. DOUGLAS POINT

A station, probably a fishing camp, is marked by many discarded shells.

124. LITTLE NECK VILLAGE

In Little Neck Village, an Indian burying place has been recently invaded by the widening of Northern Boulevard. The remains have been removed and re-buried in the churchyard of Zion Church at Douglaston. The burials indicate a settlement near by, but it may be of relatively late occupation.

128. WHITESTONE

Shell deposits indicate a fishing camp at Whitestone, which was situated on the East River, exactly opposite the large Siwanoy Village recently explored at Throg's Neck in the Borough of the Bronx.

129. COLLEGE POINT or LAWRENCE NECK

This was a village site on the Stratton property, on which burials were discovered in 1861. It is now the site of the Knickerbocker Hall. (Archeological History of New York. Albany, 1920.)

130. FLUSHING BAY

A station, probably an oystering camp.

131. POOR BOWERY

A station which is indicated by deposits of discarded shells at North Beach.

132. BOWERY ROAD, near Steinway

There was a site on which some human burials were found, on the Bowery Road. (Archeological History of New York, Albany, 1920.)

133. SANFORDS POINT, ASTORIA

A station which was marked by various Indian objects, was favorably situated on this point of land extending into the East River.

134. LONG ISLAND CITY

Human burials were found on this site in Long Island City, near Crescent Street.

65. MASPAETCHES
MASPETH

A village site near the head of Maspeth Creek, and east of Mount Zion cemetery, situated on rising ground overlooking the extensive marsh meadows bordering Newton Creek.

135. WOODHAVEN

A station, situated at Woodhaven, North Conduit, where Woodhaven Avenue connects with the Old South Road. This being inland, was probably a woodland village. Now covered with city rubbish and ashes.

136. AQUEDUCT

A site of native occupancy, was found at the Aqueduct Station, on the Old South Road, at Housatonic Street. Many fragments of pottery indicated that the clay which existed in the vicinity was utilized to make pottery vessels.

137. HAWTREE

There was a station on Hawtree Creek Road, at Flynn Avenue, where pottery sherds and a stone dish or mortar were found.

138. BERGEN CREEK

A native site, in the South Jamaica district was probably a fishing station. It was situated at the head of Bergen Creek, at Maure Avenue and Washburn Avenue, if those streets on the borough map were opened.

139. CORNELL CREEK or MAY'S LANDING

A site on the Higbie farm on Cornell Creek, South Jamaica, was probably a fishing or oystering place. It was situated at the Three Mile Road, which connects with Sutphen Road at the Rockaway Boulevard. A red stone pipe was found on this site.

140. HASSOCK CREEK

A small station at the head of Hassock Creek in Springfield, west of the Springfield Road, was marked by pottery, stone implements and knives, pitted hammer and flaked stones.

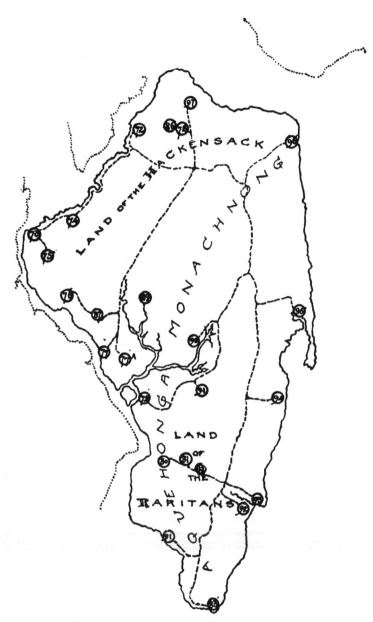

INDIAN SITES IN THE BOROUGH OF RICHMOND

INDIAN SITES IN THE BOROUGH OF RICHMOND

(The numbers are those which appear on the accompanying map)

72. PELTONS COVE

A village site at the Upper cove, West New Brighton. It is now completely covered by modern improvements. As far back as 1850, Indian burials were reported to have been disturbed there. In 1903 a few traces of native occupancy were found along the line of the Shore railroad.

73. BOWMANS BROOK

An extensive village and burial place, of apparent Hackensack occupancy, situated along the brook, sometimes known as Newtons Creek, or De Harts Brook, discharging into the Kill van Kull. This was explored in 1903 by Alanson Skinner, who found more than a hundred fire and shell-pits, and a number of human interments, with much pottery, and bone, antler, and stone implements.

74. MARINERS HARBOR

At Arlington station, a native village-site, with human interments, was discovered and explored in 1901, and further developed in 1918 by Alanson Skinner.

75. TUNISSENS NECK

Or Old Place. A native site which yielded pottery, bone, and stone objects, indicating village life.

76. WATCHOGUE

A camping site on Big Hummock, at Bloomfield, the name denoting "hill land" (Tooker, Indian Place Names). Surface discoveries indicated seasonal occupancy.

77 and 77A. LONG NECK

Now Linoleumville. A native site on the sand-dunes.

78. SILVER LAKE

A native camp-site on the shore of the lake, on which shell-pits were found.

79. FRESH KILL

At Lakes island, where there is now a garbage incinerating plant, there were many evidences of native occupancy, some having been observed by Thoreau and mentioned in his letters.

80. ROSSVILLE

A shellheap, with evidences of very ancient existence, was explored by Alanson Skinner.

81. SANDY GROUND

At Bogardus Corners. A village-site was discovered by Alanson Skinner.

82. WOODROW

Along Sandy brook there are evidences of native occupancy spread over a considerable area, apparently forming an extension of the village at Bogardus Corners.

83. WARD POINT

Near Tottenville. This very extensive native station is evidenced by masses of debris, accumulated to a considerable depth and spread irregularly over many acres. Part of the site was explored in 1898 by George H. Pepper, who discovered a number of burials, and many objects have since been unearthed through further exploration by M. R. Harrington for the Museum of the American Indian, Heye Foundation.

86. HARBOR HILL

An Indian site at the Harbor hill, at the golf links, was discovered by the explorations of Alanson Skinner.

87. CHELSEA

At the junction of the Bloomfield road and Union Avenue, a native station, with a burying-ground, existed.

89. NEW SPRINGFIELD

On Corsons brook. A site reported, but not explored.

90. SIMONSONS BROOK

On the north side of Richmond creek. At the Ketchum millpond there are evidences of an occupied station.

91. GREEN RIDGE

A site is noted by Skinner near the Richmond plank road, between Journeay Avenue and Annadale Road.

92. PRINCES BAY, PRINCESS BAY

An unexplored site at the bay, and another site marked by a shell-pit and scattered objects on the shore halfway to the lighthouse, all indicate native stations, probably for fishing purposes.

93. SEGUINE POINT

A camp-site, probably a fishing station.

94. WOODS OF ARDEN

On the shore, near the mouth of Great kills, there is a place which shows signs of native occupancy, but not of extensive character.

155

95. SHAWCOPSHEE

The modern Oakwood. The probable name of the Great kills, which may have been the refuge, for about 16 years, of the Nayack natives when they removed from Long Island. At the head of the kills are signs of occupancy, but they are not indicative of long-continued residence.

96. ARROCHAR

An ancient settlement is indicated.

97. STAPLETON

A station is recorded, but its position is indefinite.

XXXVI
EVIL DOINGS

OUR interest in the accomplishments and in the good qualities of our Indians should not lead us to ignore their known evil doings. Their social system required them to exact a full compensation for any injury, or the acceptance of a gift or an adequate payment in recompense for the injury inflicted or even for the murder of a relative or friend. If such recompense were not forthcoming, revenge, often brutal and murderous, was not only a proper act, but was an inherited obligation. This was never understood by the Dutch authorities, nor were its implications accepted, and the misunderstanding which resulted brought about much of the conflict, of the destruction and of the bloodshed that disfigured the relations between the two peoples. Let us also admit that there were among the natives some thoroughly depraved and bloodthirsty persons, whose revengeful and vicious acts brought disaster upon their own race.

While we must therefore admire their remarkable achievements under overwhelming difficulties, we may not lose sight of the deceit and dishonesty exhibited by some of their race. One such adverse opinion, describes these people as "very slovenly and nasty, stubborn, covetous, revengeful and much addicted to filching and stealing."

Yet, on the whole, they were a remarkable people who seem to have been misunderstood, often maltreated, and frquently deceived by a race possessing superior knowledge and the arts of civilization.

Hudson observed that our natives had a great prepensity for thieving, he said that they were "exceedingly adroit in carrying away whatever they take a fancy to."

The temptation to possess some of the articles which they saw on the ship, lightly regarded by the crew, was too much for those of them who had little or no respect for the right of ownership. We do not know how far this dishonesty extended in their relations with each other, that is whether the practice of stealing from one another was an established custom, but it is more than probable that he who owned anything was expected to protect it, and that he who was clever enough to abstract anything from its rightful owner was rather applauded than criticized.

Our own ancestors and perhaps all primitive peoples were so far imbued with the same principles, that the system of Anglo-Saxon jurisprudence was developed upon the theory that offences against property required greater precautions and penalties than those committed against the person.

However, among our Indians, while the crime itself may not have evoked condemnation, there was a clearly recognized method of compensation for an injury or wrong.

One of the customs of the Indian social system, which was not understood by their white contemporaries, was the duty of compensatory revenge. The system of social order which they had built up during ages of development, was the method of requiring an equivalent compensation for the commission of a crime.

The injured parties in such a case were expected to be satisfied by some payment or transfer of goods which they might accept as an equivalent for the wrong done to them. It was left to them to decide upon the extent and value of this reparation.

But if the guilty party failed to offer some form of satisfaction, revenge became a duty of the injured party which sooner or later fell upon the culprit.

A brutal Dutch settler in New Amsterdam murdered two

Indians who were bargaining with him, and stole their stock of furs.

Of the two, one had a nephew, then a young boy, to whom fell the duty of obtaining compensation or of taking revenge. Years afterwards, the nephew, then grown up, was visiting old Swits, a Dutch settler at Harlem, and was shown the old man's stock of furs. The combination of the furs and the Dutchman afforded him the opportunity of an equivalent in vengeance, whereupon he killed Swits and escaped with his stock of furs. From the Indian point of view, his act would doubtless have appeared to be entirely proper and even appropriate, and his people refused on that ground to surrender him to the Dutch authorities, the Sachem even asserting his opinion that two Dutchmen should have been killed instead of one.

An attempt to effect such a form of revengeful equivalent for the kidnapping of unsuspecting natives, is a matter of history. On the second of October, 1609, when the "Half Moon" anchored off Spuyten Duyvil there came the opportunity to the Lenape of recompense for the abduction of members of the tribe, a crime which the crew had committed upon their first contact with the natives in the lower Bay. One of those who had been thus treacherously seized by the crew, but had escaped by diving overboard, is said by Juet to have re-appeared, and accompanied by many others, approached the ship, "thinking to betray us." The crew would not permit them to gain a footing on the vessel "whereupon two canoes full of men, with their bowes and arrowes shot at us after our sterne: in recompense whereof we discharged sixe muskets and killed two or three of them."

"Then above an hundred of them came to a point of land to shoot at us." Probably Fort Washington Point, Manhattan. "There I shot a falcon at them, and killed two of them; whereupon the rest fled into the woods. Yet they manned off another canoe with nine or ten men which came to meet us. So I shot at it also a falcon,

159

and shot it through, and killed one of them. Then our men with their muskets killed three or foure more of them. So they went their way."

The blood-feud thus started brought an ample harvest of mistrust and retaliation in later years.

The principle instilled into their minds was the same as that "eye for an eye, tooth for a tooth," which is still the motive of many civilized peoples. If the enemy killed one of their own people, there was no peace until another was killed in return.

Harrington ascertained from our natives' descendants that in particularly atrocious cases, such as rape, the offender frequently met death at the hands of the victim's kinsmen, because no equivalent compensation could be offered for such a brutal crime.

No excuse can be offered, nor can any adequate explanation be made, of the frightful tortures which Indians inflicted on hapless prisoners of their own race as well as their white victims. These exhibited the brutality of the human race when uncontrolled, and it affords little extenuation to reflect that their European antagonists were often as brutal as the red men, thus requiring a revengeful equivalent, which was sometimes concentrated upon a single victim with diabolic ingenuity.

EPILOGUE

Perhaps we may derive something more than historical interest from the contemplation of the lives and doings of this humble people. We may well ask ourselves if we, under similarly prohibitive circumstances, could have hewn an existence out of the dark difficulties of primeval existence.

Amid the hardest form of living, and in spite of the driving necessity of daily hunger and thirst, complicated by the dread of the wild creatures that disputed with them the possession of the land, they developed a social system, a language, a form of art, and a religious belief. From what original degradation, from what depths of hardship and privation, the Indian had carved his way, we can only faintly imagine. But if the rough and troubled passage had proceeded that far, how much further would our Indians have advanced upon the path of progress, if their ways had not been crossed by the rough-hewn customs, the coarse habits and the intolerant beliefs of the horde of white immigrants that descended upon them.

If we regard the harsh treatment meted out to them as justified by their revengeful, cruel, and spiteful behavior, may we not ask whether there were not among the white immigrants, supposedly enlightened by civilization, the same failings.

Writing in 1765, a German merchant spoke of the natives as follows:

"In point of moderation and charity they certainly set an example to civilized peoples. When the savage has something,

161

he divides it in equal parts with his family and friends; even an apple he will cut up in six or more portions if there be so many persons present."*

Let us draw a friendly screen around their misdoings and their evil prepensities, and remember with thankfulness the obligations to them which our forbears accepted, and the benefits of which we have inherited.

Our natives have long since departed from the great metropolis, and their places are taken by a heterogeneous population, many thousandfold in number, crowded into the same space in which the natives freely wandered.

As we walk through our City's crowded ways, let us reflect that the wilderness in which it took form was in part prepared for its use by the simple people who during long centuries had made it their home.

We may find a new interest in our City's marvellous growth from those lowly conditions, if we reflect that we walk over the buried pathways the natives laid out for us, sustain ourselves by some of the food which they cultivated for us, see the same trees and plants that sheltered them, and scan the same glorious waters and the spacious ocean on which their eyes rested. Then perhaps we shall look up to the same blue sky that overhung their humble homes, and with thankful hearts follow the thought of the Indian to the Great Spirit, the creator of us all.

---

* Quoted by Albert H. Heusser in "Homes and Haunts of the Indians."

SOURCES OF INFORMATION
AND
BIBLIOGRAPHY

SOURCES OF INFORMATION and BIBLIOGRAPHY

ARMBRUSTER, EUGENE L. "The Indians of New England and New Netherlands," Brooklyn, 1918; "The Ferry Road on Long Island," Brooklyn, 1919; "Coney Island," New York, 1924.

BEAUCHAMP, PLANTAGENET. "A description of the Province of New Albion" (see 19th Annual Report of American Scenic and Historic Preservation Society), 1648.

BEAUCHAMP, W. M. "Indian Names in New York," Fayettesville, 1893; "Aboriginal Occupation of New York," N. Y. State Museum, No. 32, Albany, 1900.

BOLTON, REGINALD P. "The Indians of Washington Heights," American Museum of Natural History, New York, 1909; "Indian Paths in the Great Metropolis," Museum of the American Indian, Heye Foundation, New York, 1922; "Washington Heights, Its Eventful Past," New York, 1924; "New York City in Indian Possession," Museum American Indian, New York, 1920.

BOLTON, ROBERT. "History of the County of Westchester," Second Edition, New York, 1881.

BRINTON, DANIEL G. "A Lenape-English Dictionary," from an Anonymous M. S., probably compiled by Dencke, but in the handwriting of Rev. Kampnan, 1840, published by the Historical Society of Pennsylvania, Philadelphia, 1888; "The Lenape and Their Legends," Philadelphia, 1885."

DANKERS & SLUYTER. "Journal," Long Island Historical Society, Brooklyn, 1875.

DE LAET, JOHANNES. "New World, or Description of West India," etc., 1625.

DENTON, DANIEL. "A Brief Description of New York, 1670," London, 1701.

DE VRIES, DAVID. "Voyages from Holland to America" (Translation), 1853.

FINCH, JAMES K. "Aboriginal Remains on Manhattan Island," American Museum of Natural History, New York, 1909.

FURMAN, GABRIEL. "Antiquities of Long Island," New York, 1874.

165

GALLATIN, ALBERT. "Indian Languages," Collections of American Antiquarian Society, Cambridge, 1836; "A Synopsis of the Indian Tribes," Publication of the American Antiquarian Society, 1836.

HALL, EDWARD HAGAMAN. "New York Commercial Centenary," 19th Annual Report of the American Scenic and Historic Preservation Society, 1914.

HARRINGTON, M. R. "American Anthropologist," Vol. X, No. 3, 1908 and Vol. XV, No. 2, 1913.

HAYNES, H. W. "The Bow and Arrow," Boston Society Natural History, Vol. XXIII, Boston.

HECKEWELDER, JOHN G. E. "History, Manners and Customs of the Indian Nations," Philadelphia, 1876; "The Languages of the American Indians," Trans. of the American Philosophical Society, 1816.

HEUSSER, ALBERT H. "Homes and Haunts of the Indians."

HODGE, FREDERICK W. "Handbook of the American Indian," Bureau of American Ethnology, Washington, 1911.

HUDSON, HENRY. "Journal." See 15th Annual Report, American Scenic and Historic Preservation Society, New York, 1912.

JOHNSON, AMANDUS. "Geographia Americæ," 1925.

MICHAELIUS, REV. JONAS. "Year Book of Collegiate Reformed Protestant Dutch Church in the City of New York, No. 17," 1896; Trans. of the New York Historical Society, 1880.

MUNSELL. "Annals of Albany," Vol. II.

O'CALLAGHAN, E. B. "Documentary History of New York," Albany, 1863-7.

OGILBY, JOHN. "America," being the latest and most accurate description of the New World, London, 1671.

PARKER, ARTHUR C. "The Archæological History of New York," State Report 2 Vols., Albany, 1920.

RUTTENBER. "History of the Indian Tribes of the Hudson River," Albany, 1872.

SCHOOLCRAFT, HENRY R. "Aboriginal Names and Geographical Terminology of the State of New York." Trans. New York Historical Society, 1844-5.

SKINNER, ALANSON. "Archæology of Manhattan Island," American Museum of Natural History, New York, 1909; "Exploration of Aboriginal Sites, Clason Point and Schley Avenue," Museum of the American Indian, Heye Foundation, New York, 1919; "Notes on Mahikan Ethnology," Pub. Museum of the City of Milwaukee, Milwaukee, 1925; "The Indians of Manhattan

Island and Vicinity," American Museum of Natural History, New York; "The Lenape Indians of Staten Island," New York, 1909.

TOOKER, WILLIAM W. "The Indian Place-Names on Long Island," New York, 1911.

TRUMBULL, JAMES H. "Indian Names of Connecticut," Hartford, 1881.

VAN DER DONCK, ADRIAEN. "The Representations of New Netherland, 1656," New York Historical Society, Vol. 1, New York.

VAN WASSENAER, NICHOLAS. "Historisch van Europa," 1621-1631; "Narratives of New Netherland," J. F. Jameson.

WILLIAMS, ROGER. "A Key Into the Languages of America," London, 1643.

WISSLER, CLARK. "Anthropological Papers," American Museum of Natural History, New York, 1909.

WOLLEY, CHARLES. "A Two-Year Journal in New York," London, 1701.